RECIPE

SECRETS TO RUNNING A PROFITABLE

FOR

AND SUSTAINABLE BUSINESS

SUCCESS

WRITTEN BY

JOS SALDANA

Restaurant Killers ®

To the woman who has been my unwavering rock and guiding light, this book is dedicated to you. My dear mother, you have always been there for me, even during my darkest moments. You never gave up on me, and you never stopped pushing me to pursue my passions and reach for the stars. Your unconditional love and unwavering support have been the foundation of my success and the driving force behind my dreams. I am forever grateful for your faith in me, your endless encouragement, and your unwavering belief that I can achieve anything I set my mind to. Thank you for allowing me to dream and live my life on my own terms. This book is for you, Mom, and for the infinite love and inspiration you continue to give me.

Contents

Prologue

Picture this: a young and ambitious entrepreneur with big dreams of bringing a culinary piece of his beloved Chicago to the bustling city of Mexico City. He was full of hope and excitement, eager to thrive in his new restaurant business venture. Little did he know that the road ahead would be filled with twists and turns and the challenges he would encounter would test his resolve and push him to the brink.

As a complete novice in the Food and Beverage industry, our protagonist had no idea what was in store for him. Armed with nothing but determination and an unwavering can-do attitude, he set out to replicate the success of a well-known and established Chicago franchise but in a brand new international location, Mexico City. He had heard stories of other restaurateurs who had made it big without much experience in business, finance, or management, so what could possibly go wrong?

As it turns out, everything.

Opening a restaurant in a foreign country turned out to be one of the most difficult and rewarding experiences of his life. From navigating unfamiliar regulations and adapting to a new business culture to being sued for intellectual property rights by the largest restaurant group in Latin America, this endeavor was a true test of his determination and resilience both personally and professionally. But through it all, he never gave up. He persevered, learning from mistakes along the way, and overcoming the odds to achieve success beyond his wildest dreams.

Through this book, our now accomplished entrepreneur shares his experiences and the hard-earned lessons he's learned while marketing, operating, and scaling a franchise, in the hopes that it will help others be better equipped while navigating their own business. Whether you're a seasoned business owner or just starting out, this book is a must-read for anyone who wants to achieve success in the Food and Beverage industry. With insider secrets and personal anecdotes, this book includes valuable insights into what it takes to start, grow, and advance your business.

Join our protagonist on his journey and discover the secrets to his success. Who knows? You might just find the inspiration and motivation you need to take your business to new heights, and even new countries.

Introduction

Have you ever dreamed of owning a restaurant? Have you ever wondered why some restaurants succeed over others? Are you excited to make your mark in the culinary world but don't know where to begin? Do you have a restaurant but feel like you've had to sacrifice your personal life in order to succeed? If so, then look no further than this book! I've been in your shoes before. I know firsthand the pitfalls and mistakes that can often lead to the downfall of even the most promising restaurant.

Before embarking on my journey, I had witnessed the glamor and heard countless stories of life as a successful restaurateur, so when I had the opportunity to be part of this industry, I immediately took it. My journey began with a relentless and never ending pursuit towards achieving "success." After nearly a decade of starting my journey I can proudly say that I am now officially a restaurateur. Sounds fancy, right? Little do most people know, however, that this title was hard earned, through investing blood, sweat and tears, in order to build a profitable and sustainable business.

In this book, I share my personal experiences and industry specific insights so you can avoid these common traps. I have learned valuable lessons that have shaped my approach to running a business and I'm eager to share these insider secrets with you in the hopes that they will inspire you to open a business and reach new heights of success.

So is there a magic formula for success? What is the secret to success in the restaurant industry? It's not really about doing things differently; it's about doing the same things but in a strategic way. Let's begin with the basics of business. It is commonly known there are five essential elements to succeeding in this industry: location, menu planning, customer experience, owner participation, and marketing. In this book, however, we will only explore these elements on a superficial level. While they are essential for running a successful restaurant business, from the importance of choosing the right location to the power of a well-engineered menu to the crucial role of exceptional customer service, these are just the basics of any business and there is already plenty of information available on those topics. What makes this book unique is that it delves into the insider secrets that nobody else in the industry is talking about - the often overlooked, but extremely powerful truths that will truly make a difference. Owning and running a restaurant is no easy feat, but with the right mindset and strategic approach, it can be a highly rewarding and profitable experience.

Chapter 1: Passion Alone is not Enough

The restaurant industry can seem exciting and full of promise, many aspiring restaurateurs enter the field for their love of food and hospitality and the desire to share part of themselves with the world. However, passion alone is not enough. It is critical to understand that the restaurant business is, first and foremost, a business. That means the profitability of your restaurant comes down to your bottom line, you must be able to manage your finances, understand your customer and position yourself in a way that stands out from the competition.

While passion and creativity are important, they must be paired with strategic thinking and planning to achieve success. It is crucial to engage in thorough research and planning before opening a restaurant. Without a solid business plan, a carefully crafted menu, and an understanding of the market and the competition, a restaurant is likely to struggle to survive. This chapter aims to guide you through the essential steps of research and planning before embarking on the journey of opening your restaurant.

Market Research

When I decided to open up my first restaurant, I did so by taking a successful local restaurant franchise in the United States and expanding it to the Latin American market. For me, the allure of this ambitious endeavor could be summed up in one word: Opportunity. This expansion to Mexico tapped into a growing demand for American-style cuisine in the region, and offered a unique and familiar dining experience that clearly set the brand apart from its local competitors.

Although expanding a business into a global market is exciting, it is also a significant undertaking that requires extensive market research. It wasn't enough to simply know the restaurant concept was successful in its home country; I needed to understand the unique challenges and opportunities that came with growing into a completely new country. The first crucial step in opening a successful restaurant is conducting thorough market research and analysis. Without a clear understanding of the market and its trends, a restaurant can quickly find itself struggling to attract customers and remain profitable. Market research involves gathering information about the market, competitors, and target customers to identify opportunities and assess demand for a particular type of cuisine or restaurant concept. By analyzing this data, a restaurateur can develop a clearer understanding of the market and its trends, and identify gaps that can be profited from. This analysis will also help you make informed decisions around menu design, pricing, and marketing strategies.

I spent countless hours researching different markets, analyzing consumer behavior, and developing a comprehensive business plan. One of the first tools I used in market research was a SWOT analysis, which stands for strengths, weaknesses, opportunities, and threats. This analysis helps to identify the internal strengths and weaknesses of a restaurant, as well as the external opportunities and threats that it faces. Other tools I utilized included customer surveys, focus groups, and competitor analysis, all of which provided valuable insights into the Mexican market and helped me make informed decisions moving forward.

Through my research, I discovered that the key to success for this expansion was having a thorough understanding of the new market. This meant not only understanding the cultural nuances and preferences of the target audience but also the legal and regulatory environment of the new market. It is vital to understand the idiosyncrasies and consumer behavior of the region before diving in.

Expanding to Latin America was a bold and risky endeavor- even more than I had originally anticipated. While speaking the language and looking the part certainly helped, it's so much more than that. Latin America is a region made up of diverse countries with their own unique cultures and consumption habits. Therefore, to achieve success, you must develop differentiated and innovative strategies tailored to each market. Expanding into a new market is an opportunity to learn about a new culture, meet new people, and grow your business in ways you never thought possible.

So, if you're thinking about an international expansion, remember to take the time to plan carefully. Set clear objectives, analyze your resources, and be prepared to adapt your strategy as needed. With a structured plan and an open mind, you'll be well on your way to success in the global market.

Business Planning

Another critical aspect to cover in this first phase is business planning. Ask yourself the tough questions: What do I want to achieve? What are my company's long-term goals? Is a global expansion aligned with my company's overarching vision? Is it better to join a franchise model or can I start my own business and brand? These are just a few examples, but the point is to be specific about your objectives.

Once you've established your objectives, it's essential to analyze the resources required to achieve them. This means taking a close look at your finances, human resources, and technology. You need to determine what resources you'll need to carry out the project and start operations.

It's also essential to challenge everything along the way. Don't be afraid to question your assumptions, your business model, and your strategy. Ask yourself, "What if this doesn't work? What if our plan needs to change?" This approach will ensure you end up with a well structured plan that takes into account all possible scenarios and sets you up for higher probabilities of success. I know this may not seem like the exercise you want to go through when you are excited and hopeful that your concept is brilliant, unique, and born to be successful, but trust me, I've been there and I quickly learned that business planning is everything. The best time to account for the unexpected is during the planning stage.

Take your time and research everything, challenge everything. The planning stage will set your foundation for success.

As an entrepreneur, I always thought I had everything under control. I was diligent in my research, I had a solid business plan and an innovative marketing strategy. But little did I know that one crucial element could bring my thriving restaurant business in Mexico to a screeching halt. I failed to ask myself the tough questions, for example, the possibility of starting with a new standalone concept, rather than bringing an established franchise. I never considered this possibility until it was too late.

Let me explain. You may remember I mentioned I brought a successful local franchise to Mexico. Now, don't get me wrong, franchises can be very successful because they offer small businesses access to economies of scale without requiring large financial investments. With the support of an established brand, entrepreneurs can carve out a niche for themselves in the market and increase their chances of success. It seemed like a no-brainer to align myself with a franchise model when I decided to open my restaurant. However, in my particular situation, I didn't benefit from any of the advantages that come with being a part of a franchise but was left with all the disadvantages associated with it.

The original business model had proven to be a hit in Chicago, but it had yet to be successful outside of the local market. We were pioneers, venturing to prove an American concept in Mexico for the first time. To begin with, brand recognition, while very strong in its local country, was non-existent at a global scale. So we had to position a brand new concept both online and offline with limited resources. We didn't have the structure, resources, or human capital to deploy a comprehensive marketing campaign.

The long distance from the Chicago-based company made support virtually non-existent. So with little, to no support, we had to build the infrastructure of the brand from the ground up. The training and support were there in theory, but in practice, we had to adapt and modify the operation, human resources, and training manuals to adhere to the customs and unique laws and regulations of Mexico. The economies of scale didn't work in our favor either, rather than having the usual advantages of buying power and reduced costs, we were treated as a brand-new concept trying to prove its worth to suppliers in Mexico City.

In summary, we didn't enjoy any of the brand recognition, competitive advantage, marketing capital, training, support, infrastructure, proven business model, or economies of scale that one could expect from a typical franchise expansion. Instead, we had to deal with the biggest drawbacks of joining a franchise model, which is lack of control and high costs. As a franchisee, you are required to follow the franchisor's rules and regulations, which can limit your ability to make your own decisions about your restaurant. This can be frustrating if you have a specific vision or want to try out new ideas. The most draining aspect, however, is the high costs. Sometimes these costs can be justified when you have all the advantages of being part of a franchise model. In my situation, joining a franchise was an expensive lesson, with initial franchise fees, ongoing royalties, and other costs that ate into our profits and made it more challenging to achieve financial success.

My advice is, if you're considering opening a restaurant, or any business, think carefully about whether the proposed business model is right for you. Don't assume that it's a clear path to success.

Starting a stand-alone, brand-new concept can be challenging, but with the right team, innovative marketing strategies, and a clear vision, it can be done. Further chapters will explore each of these topics extensively, providing in-depth analysis and tips.

Location Selection

As we dive deeper into the intricacies of planning, we encounter a decisive milestone that shapes the destiny of a restaurateur- the selection of the perfect location. I can't stress enough the importance of this step. You've probably heard the saying a thousand times: "Location, location, location." But what does it truly mean for us in the restaurant industry? It holds a similar significance as it does in the world of real estate, where the physical location of a property can make or break its value. Likewise, the location of a restaurant plays a vital role in determining its success. I learned this lesson the hard way when I opened my first flagship location in the most touristy area in the heart of Mexico City, without doing enough research into the surrounding area. It was a hip and bustling area, but it was also saturated with competition and although it had plenty of foot traffic the size of the space and price per square foot simply didn't make any business sense. I quickly learned that being in a cool area doesn't always translate to a successful business. In a subsequent chapter, we will analyze the intricate relationship between location choice and its impact on your bottom line, but for now, let's talk about the key points that you should consider when making this important decision.

So, how do you choose the right location for your restaurant? There are many factors to consider. One crucial factor is foot traffic. You want to be in an area with high foot traffic, but not necessarily where your restaurant is competing with many other establishments. It's important to find a balance between visibility and competition. Accessibility is another important factor. Is your restaurant easily accessible by car or public transportation? Is there ample parking nearby? These are all factors that can affect the number of customers that come through your door. In addition to these factors, there are several other considerations to keep in mind when choosing a location, such as local zoning laws, building regulations, and neighborhood demographics. Finally, it's also important to think about the long-term potential of a location. Is the area likely to continue to grow and develop, or is it in decline? Are there any upcoming developments or changes that could impact your business? These are all questions to consider when choosing a location.

Let's explore an analogy to grasp the true essence of this concept. Picture two restaurants, Restaurant A and Restaurant B. Both establishments have talented chefs, mouthwatering menus, and a true commitment to exceptional customer service. However, their divergent locations set them on contrasting paths. Restaurant A finds its home in the heart of a bustling downtown area—a vibrant hub surrounded by offices, shopping centers, and entertainment venues. Meanwhile, Restaurant B sets up shop in a cozy corner of a quiet suburban neighborhood, with limited visibility and fewer passersby.

Now, both restaurants offer exceptional dining experiences, but Restaurant A has a clear advantage thanks to its prime location. Situated downtown, it benefits from a constant stream of foot traffic—people bustling about, looking for a quick bite or a memorable dining experience. Easy parking options and accessibility add to its charm, making it a convenient choice for many. Plus, the diverse population in the area perfectly aligns with the cuisine and atmosphere that Restaurant A offers, attracting its ideal clientele effortlessly.

On the other hand, Restaurant B faces its fair share of challenges due to its location. Nestled in the peaceful suburbs, it struggles to attract a consistent flow of customers without the benefit of foot traffic. Relying primarily on local residents, it finds itself relying on their loyalty and word-of-mouth recommendations. To truly thrive, Restaurant B needs to get creative with marketing strategies and find ways to stand out from the competition in the area. By doing your due diligence and carefully considering all the factors, you can strategically set your restaurant up for success.

Financial Planning

The next phase in the planning process is financial planning. Financial planning is an aspect that is often underestimated, at its core, it is about creating a roadmap for your restaurant's financial success. As aspiring restaurant owners, you may have grand ideas for your restaurant's menu, decor, and ambiance but may overlook the importance of creating a realistic budget. Without careful financial planning, a restaurant owner's dreams can quickly turn into a financial nightmare and you might find yourself juggling insufficient funds right from the start. Achieving success in the restaurant industry requires aspiring owners to have a firm grasp on the critical components of financial planning, including creating a realistic budget for day-to-day operations and forecasting revenue and expenses.

When it comes to creating a budget, it's crucial to start with a detailed list of all potential expenses. To do so you must first consider the size and location of your restaurant. For example, a restaurant in a high-end neighborhood may require a larger budget than a small cafe in a less affluent area. It's essential to factor in all potential expenses, this includes both fixed and variable costs. Fixed costs are expenses that remain the same, such as rent, insurance, loan payments, utilities, equipment, and marketing. Variable costs, on the other hand, are expenses that can fluctuate, such as food costs and labor. In chapter six, we will explore costs in greater depth, thoroughly examining and analyzing this significant component. It's also important to account for unexpected expenses that may arise, such as repairs or emergency situations. You should create a contingency fund in your budget to cover these unforeseen costs. Once all potential expenses have been identified, you can begin to create a detailed budget. You should also factor in the revenue you expect to generate and create a plan to monitor and adjust their budget as needed.

To illustrate the importance of creating a realistic budget, look at what happened to the restaurant industry as a result of COVID. Restaurant owners who created a comprehensive budget and were meticulous in their financial planning were able to navigate unexpected expenses, weather the economic downturn, and keep their businesses afloat. Creating a realistic budget is a key aspect to set up your business for success.

Forecasting revenue and expenses is another critical aspect of financial planning. It is like the crystal ball of financial planning for your restaurant. By delving into past data, observing market trends, and leveraging industry knowledge, you can make educated predictions about your future income and expenses. At the core of successful financial planning lies the ability to project revenue accurately. Market research becomes an invaluable tool in this process, empowering you to make informed decisions. Understanding your target audience and their preferences can help you develop a menu that appeals to them and set prices that are competitive in the market. Analyzing sales data from similar establishments in the area can also give you an idea of what you can expect in terms of revenue.

Pricing strategies can also play a significant role in revenue forecasting. Will you offer happy hour specials or promotions to drive traffic during slower times? How will you balance affordability with profitability? Proper financial planning will help you find that sweet spot between pricing too low and struggling to make ends meet, or pricing too high and driving customers away. It's a delicate balance that can make all the difference in the success of your restaurant.

In addition to revenue, projecting expenses is equally important. Resource allocation is a key aspect that financial planning addresses. Allocating your resources, like funds, staff, and inventory, without a plan can be a recipe for disaster. Labor costs are typically the biggest expense for restaurants, and accurately forecasting these costs is critical. Consider factors such as staffing levels, wages, and benefits when projecting labor expenses. Inventory and food costs are another significant expense for restaurants. Menu planning is fundamental for this and it goes beyond simply creating a tempting menu. By finalizing your menu and listing all the dishes and their ingredients, including the quantities required for each recipe, you lay the groundwork for estimating your inventory and food costs.

Effective inventory management is essential to minimize waste and control costs. Waste or shortages can occur when you don't know how to distribute these resources efficiently. When it comes to inventory management, two key factors to consider are inventory turnover and par levels. Specifying how frequently you aim to sell and replenish your inventory within a specific time period. Next, set par levels for each ingredient based on your sales projections, desired inventory turnover, and delivery frequency. These par levels act as the minimum stock quantity required before reordering. Finally, marketing expenses should also be factored into your financial projections. Determine how much you will need to invest in advertising and promotions to build awareness and attract customers to your establishment.

Are you already overwhelmed? That wasn't the idea. The point is merely to show you how passion and love for your craft alone is not enough to ensure your success in the restaurant industry. It is essential to balance passion with careful planning, research, and financial analysis. If you are considering opening a restaurant or taking your restaurant to a new market, don't underestimate the power of planning. Take all the time you need to do it before you open your restaurant; I cannot stress this enough, you must prepare if you want to succeed.

Planning is not a one-time thing. It's an ongoing process that requires you to stay flexible and adaptable. I like to review my goals, celebrate my milestones, analyze my failures, regroup and plan accordingly on a yearly basis. You need to be willing to pivot if things aren't working out as planned. Keep an eye on your objectives, and if they're no longer relevant, don't be afraid to adjust them.

Planning can seem overwhelming, but it doesn't have to be. When I first started, I remember feeling like I was in over my head. But I learned that taking things one step at a time made the process more manageable. Break down your plan into smaller, more achievable goals, and celebrate your successes along the way. My experience has taught me that planning is crucial when expanding internationally, but it's not everything. You also need to be adaptable, open-minded, and willing to learn.

As you embark on your journey in the restaurant industry, remember that it takes more than passion to succeed. A successful opening or expansion is linked directly to a well-thought-out plan.

34

Chapter 2:

Risks are Necessary

Thriving in the restaurant industry requires a bold spirit and a willingness to take risks. Running a restaurant is not a journey for the faint of heart—it demands significant investments of time, money, and energy. However, it is through calculated risks that restaurateurs can unlock substantial rewards. In this chapter, we will take a plunge into the art of embracing calculated risks, recognizing opportunities, and conquering challenges to establish a thriving restaurant business. We will also explore the inherent benefits and potential drawbacks of risk-taking, equipping you with proven strategies to minimize risk and maximize the potential for success. By the conclusion of this chapter, you will possess the tools and knowledge to take calculated risks that will lead to increased profitability, customer satisfaction, and overall success in the restaurant industry.

Let's begin with a question, what prevents us from taking risks? For most people is fear, fear of failure. The fear of failure is a common roadblock that many aspiring entrepreneurs face when considering taking risks. The fear of not succeeding can prevent individuals from pursuing their dreams and realizing their full potential. In the realm of the restaurant industry, the fear of failure can have a paralyzing effect on aspiring entrepreneurs, creating an atmosphere of doubt and hesitation. This fear is rooted in two significant factors: the industry's well-known high rate of failure and the considerable financial investment needed to bring a restaurant to life. Compounding this fear is the pressure of societal expectations, which adds an extra layer of anxiety for those embarking on their restaurant journey. We are often conditioned to believe that success is measured by material possessions and financial wealth. As a result, the pressure to succeed can be overwhelming, and the fear of failure can prevent us from taking risks that could lead to success. Personal insecurities can also play a significant role in the fear of failure. Many aspiring restaurateurs may feel they lack the necessary skills, experience, or resources to succeed. This self-doubt can lead to procrastination, indecision, and analysis paralysis, preventing them from taking the necessary steps to achieve their goals and can even deter them from pursuing their dreams entirely. They may find themselves waiting for the "perfect" moment to take action. However, the truth is that there is never a perfect time, and waiting for too long can lead to missed opportunities.

Indecision is another way in which the fear of failure can manifest itself. The restaurant industry requires entrepreneurs to make many decisions before opening and on a daily basis. The fear of making the wrong decision can lead to indecision and prevent entrepreneurs from moving forward. Finally, analysis paralysis can also result from the fear of failure. Overthinking and analyzing every decision can lead to a state of analysis paralysis, where entrepreneurs are unable to make any decisions at all.

Overcoming Fear

Let's discuss three practical strategies for overcoming this fear. The first strategy in overcoming the fear of failure is to reframe failure as a learning opportunity. Rather than seeing failure as a setback, successful restaurateurs view it as a chance to learn and grow. They understand that failure is an inevitable part of the learning process and embrace it as a necessary step on the path to success. Another key strategy for overcoming the fear of failure is to develop a growth mindset. A growth mindset is the belief that our abilities and intelligence can be developed through hard work, dedication, and a willingness to learn. Successful restaurateurs with a growth mindset are not afraid to take risks because they understand that failure is not a reflection of their abilities, but rather an opportunity to learn and grow. Finally, it's important to surround yourself with a supportive network of family, friends, and colleagues who believe in you and your vision. When you're feeling discouraged or fearful, turn to your support system for encouragement and motivation. Remember, success is not achieved overnight, but rather through hard work, perseverance, and a willingness to take risks.

The REAACT Test

If you were to ask me what the key to my success is, I will tell you that it's the ability to take risks. Risks are a necessary part of the game, and without them, it's impossible to grow and evolve. However, taking risks doesn't mean you should take a blind leap of faith. Instead, it's about taking calculated risks that pay off and help your brand stand out from the competition. To take calculated risks, you need to be innovative and flexible, and create a clear plan.

Taking risks can be an effective way to grow your business and achieve success, but it's important to consider several factors to determine if a risk is a good idea.

When deciding whether to take risks, I use a test I created called the REAACT Test. This test allows me the opportunity to measure its probability of success.

Research: The first step is to conduct thorough research to understand the market and identify trends and opportunities. This information can help you make informed decisions about the risk you want to take.

Evaluate: Next, evaluate the resources available to support the risk, including financial, personnel, and other resources. Determine if you have the necessary resources to support the risk, and if not, identify ways to obtain them.

Analyze: Perform a cost-benefit analysis to evaluate the potential benefits and risks of the decision and determine if the benefits outweigh the costs. It's important to weigh the potential risks against the potential rewards.

Align: Considering whether the risk is truly aligned with your overall business strategy and goals. Taking a risk that doesn't align with your strategy can have negative consequences.

Create: Create a contingency plan to mitigate any negative consequences that may arise from the risk. This can help you manage the risk and minimize the impact on your business.

Time: Lastly, consider the timing of the risk and whether it's the right time to take it. Timing can impact the success of the risk, and taking a risk too early or too late can have negative consequences.

Taking calculated risks is about having a clear understanding of your brand's strengths and weaknesses, as well as the competitive landscape of the market you're entering. Starbucks is a great example of a company that took a calculated risk to expand its business internationally. The company had to adjust its menu and store design to cater to Japanese tastes and preferences when it opened its first store outside of North America in Tokyo, Japan, in 1996. The risk paid off, and Starbucks has since expanded to over 80 countries worldwide, becoming one of the world's most recognized brands.

Innovation and creativity are also essential when taking calculated risks. Spotify disrupted the music industry by offering a new way for consumers to access and discover music. In 2013, Spotify took a calculated risk by expanding into the Latin

American market, which was dominated by local streaming services. To differentiate itself from competitors, Spotify offered localized playlists and worked with local artists to promote its service. The strategy paid off, and Spotify became the top music streaming service in Latin America.

In the restaurant industry, we learn the value of taking risks with simple moves like introducing a new dish on the menu. We want to showcase our unique flavors or creative cuisine. A new dish can be a bold move, because we are unsure how it will be received. But if executed properly, this calculated risk can pay off, and it can quickly become the most popular dish on the menu. Another example of a calculated risk that restaurateurs take on a daily basis is adjusting pricing for certain menu items. Let's say you are considering raising the prices of one of your dishes due to increasing ingredient costs. If you properly analyze and assess this move, you can get back on track with running a profitable business.

In my journey as a restaurateur one of the biggest risks I've taken was without a doubt deciding to expand to Mexico. I knew I was in for a challenge introducing a unique product to a brand new audience. As I embarked on this journey with my team, it was clear that we needed a well-thought-out plan and a dash of audacity to make our mark. Taking calculated risks and embracing innovative marketing strategies became our guiding principles.

We knew that just being different from the competition wouldn't be enough. We needed to give them an experience that was truly authentic and would make them understand why our product was so special. To achieve our goal, the first step was to preserve the unique identity of our star dish. So, we set out to recreate it in our new international location, by carefully sourcing the same high-quality ingredients used in our Chicago locations. Additionally, we dedicated ourselves to training our new team to prepare this signature dish with the same exacting standards that have earned it its reputation.

Once we accomplished this milestone, our focus shifted to establishing standardized procedures and recipes, ensuring unwavering consistency in the quality of our star product. While some kitchen enthusiasts and chefs may hold differing opinions, the undeniable truth remains: consistency is vital for authenticity. Customers expect to relish the same exceptional experience and standards during each visit to our restaurant. Not only does this foster loyalty, but it also brings about significant food cost benefits, a topic we will go into in further detail in later chapters. We had the product, we had the standards. All that was left was training our Front of House staff on what made us truly special and empower them to share this knowledge with our customers.

Our staff became our brand ambassadors, representing the heart and soul of our restaurant. We invested time and effort into educating them about the story behind our star dish, the passion that went into crafting it, and the unique elements that set us apart from the competition. And it paid off, we opened our doors to a crowd of curious customers, and before long, we were on a line serving up our star dish that was every bit as delicious as what you would find in Chicago. This experience taught us that no matter where you are in the world, if you can create a truly authentic experience for your customers, they will appreciate it, and they will come back again and again. It's about more than just educating your customers- it's about creating a connection with them that goes beyond the product.

Marketing Strategies

But authenticity alone was not enough. We also needed to be innovative and bold in our marketing strategies and we knew that digital marketing and social media would be a key component. In preparation for our grand opening, we devised an ingenious guerilla marketing strategy tailored to resonate with our audience and create a buzz of organic digital and social media content. Our opening weekend coincided with the romantic holiday of Valentine's Day, and we embraced this opportunity to spread love and showcase our "With love from Chicago" campaign. Armed with batches of delicious homemade cookies, we went to some of the city's main parks, eager to spread the love and introduce our brand to the world. The concept was simple yet effective: we offered free cookies to every couple, friends, or soon-to-be couples who shared love with one another or even with one of our team members. The cookies themselves became the ambassadors of our identity, as discreetly nestled within each label they could easily find our webpage and social media handles, subtly inviting curious minds to explore more.

The impact of our guerrilla marketing was undeniable. Our social media followers skyrocketed by the thousands, and in the days that followed, as the excitement and curiosity spread, our restaurant saw an influx of eager customers seeking to experience firsthand what we had to offer.

But we didn't stop there. We understood the significance of word-of-mouth marketing as a driving force to our success. To harness this powerful tool, we crafted a strategy that would not only captivate our customers but also foster a genuine connection with our brand. So we got creative and started offering monthly cooking classes that allowed our customers to get a behind-the-scenes feel for our star product. This class quickly became a sensation as new customers were excited about the opportunity to not only get to try the product but learn how to make it. Through the success of this initiative, we witnessed firsthand the profound impact of engaging with our customers on a deeper level. This bold and innovative strategy not only solidified our presence in the new market but also built a loyal customer base.

Digital marketing quickly became an essential and integral part of the growth and success of our brand. It was evident that we needed to craft a compelling online presence that spoke directly to our audience. With this in mind, we devoted ourselves to create a unique website exclusively tailored to our international location. A virtual space with photos, collaborations and engaging videos, each capturing our processes from start to finish. Additionally, we understood the importance of being visible to our potential customers. So, we optimized our website for search engines to ensure that when people in our new market searched for strategic words about our product or Chicago, our website would come up at the top of the search results. But digital marketing didn't end there; it was an unfolding story across various platforms. We created new Facebook, Instagram, and Google My Business accounts to share photos of our products, behind-the-scenes footage of our kitchen, and testimonials from satisfied customers. These basics were at the heart of our digital journey, providing a sturdy foundation for all our strategies to thrive. Each element, from fine-tuning our website to crafting captivating social media stories, played a vital role in shaping the story of our brand. Yet, in the vast and competitive realm of social media, we knew we needed to stand out from the crowd. To make our mark and stand out we courageously embraced risks and created posts that pushed the boundaries and captured the attention of our target audience.

Five Social Media Tips

Embracing risk in the world of social media opens up a world of possibilities, where posts come in all shapes and sizes – from controversial opinions to witty one-liners. Picture yourself scrolling through your social media feed and stumbling upon a post that makes you stop, laugh, or even gasp in astonishment. These moments of intrigue and captivation are precisely what you should aspire to create. So, if you're seeking to elevate your social media game, here are five tips I used to create engaging and memorable posts that increased our brand awareness and followers:

1. Know Your Audience: First and foremost, it is crucial to know your audience. Conduct market research to understand their interests, pain points, and values. Once you know what resonates with them, you can tailor your posts accordingly.

2. Authenticity is Key: Don't be afraid to share your true opinions, even if they are controversial. Your audience will appreciate your honesty and connect with you on a deeper level.

3. Leverage Humor: Use humor to inject personality and warmth into your brand. Humor is a powerful tool that can help you create memorable and shareable posts.

4. Take Calculated Risks: While risky posts can help you stand out, it's important to avoid posts that

could offend or alienate your audience. Always be mindful of your brand image and values.

5. Engage With Your Audience: Once you've created risky posts, respond to comments and messages, and ask for feedback to show that you value their opinions.

As simple as these tips may sound, I can vouch from personal experience that even the most creative team can encounter challenges when consistently churning out content. In the dynamic world of digital marketing, a bold move can sometimes take an unexpected turn, putting your brand to the test. Being prepared to seize such opportunities and navigate through them becomes crucial to preserving your brand's identity. To bring this to life, let me share an example from our very own adventure. We compared our star product to a classic Mexican street dish in a Facebook post, rating them with emojis. The post became a hit, receiving 1000+ likes and hundreds of comments in less than eight hours. Some people in Mexico were offended and attacked us in the comments, accusing us of throwing shade at their ancestral cuisine, which was factually inaccurate. But we didn't let that stop us. We kept the conversation going, engaging with our audience, even with our biggest haters.

Our success wasn't the likes, it was the engagement we had with our audience. We made it fun, we kept it light, and we stayed authentic to our brand. If they complained about the price, we matched our price to our competitor's, if they complained about convenience and proximity to their location, we paid for our customers' Uber rides, and if they insisted the competitor's product was better we challenged them to a live taste test party with their friends. We turned our haters into our biggest fans, all because we took a risk and stayed true to our brand. So go ahead, take a risk, it can be one of the best ways to create a strong brand identity and engage with your followers on a deeper level.

The Power of Alliances

Finally and most importantly, when it comes to getting the word out, your biggest ally is the media. That's why, as part of our initial marketing strategy, we decided to reach out to the local media. We invited food critics and bloggers to come and try our product, and we even offered special promotions and discounts to our early customers to encourage them to spread the word. Turning to influencer marketing helped us reach a wider audience. We partnered with popular food bloggers, strategic media alliances, and Instagrammers in our new market who shared their experiences and helped introduce their followers to our product. And let me tell you, these strategies paid off big time. Our name quickly spread throughout the local community and beyond, and we became one of the most talked-about restaurants in the area.

Looking back on our success, I can honestly say that our media alliances were instrumental in getting us to where we were. By strategically positioning our brand in the market and leveraging the power of influencer marketing, we were able to reach a wider audience and build a loyal customer base.

So if you're starting a new business or looking to take your existing one to the next level, my advice to you is simple: don't underestimate the power of the media.

When it comes to reaching out to media, Instagrammers, and bloggers for your restaurant, don't be afraid to take risks and take a little leap of faith. Trust me, I know it can be nerve-wracking, but sometimes the best opportunities come from embracing a little risk. It might feel like you're putting yourself out there, but that's where the magic happens. You'll see, these media folks and social media stars are always on the lookout for something exciting and fresh; the media appreciates authenticity and creativity. Remember, it's all about showing the world what makes your restaurant special and how much passion goes into every plate you serve. So, don't hesitate to be different, be genuine, and be yourself. You never know, that little risk you took might just open doors to incredible opportunities.

Taking risks can be scary but it is also essential for growth and success. But taking risks doesn't mean being reckless. It's important to take calculated risks and be strategic in your approach. To truly take calculated risks, you need to do your research and understand the consumer preferences in the new market. But more importantly, you need to be flexible and adaptable in order to meet the needs of that market.

When I took a risk and launched my restaurant in a new market, I knew it was a calculated risk, but I was also flexible and adaptable in adjusting my product and marketing approach. And it paid off. So, if you're thinking about taking a risk in your own business, my advice is to go for it. But remember to test your initiative using the REAACT test. Be strategic, flexible, and adaptable along the way. Take risks that align with your goals and values, and don't be afraid to pivot if needed. As entrepreneurs, we must always be willing to take risks and push ourselves out of our comfort zones. It's not always easy, but the rewards can be great. I encourage you to take a leap of faith and see where it takes you. Who knows, it might just be the best decision you ever make.

Chapter 3:
Build Trust

As we begin this chapter and prepare to delve deeper into the essence of running a successful business in the forthcoming sections, I am excited to impart a priceless lesson I have gained through my own personal experiences- a secret ingredient for success that surpasses any conventional business wisdom: the importance of building trust. Trust serves as the bedrock upon which all prosperous relationships are built. It forms the very foundation that enables you to establish meaningful connections with all the relationships your business engages in, including business partners, suppliers, customers, and most importantly, your staff.

Without trust, gaining a foothold in the market will remain an ongoing challenge.

Now, you may wonder, why is trust so vital in the realm of restaurant entrepreneurship, especially when venturing into foreign territories with diverse cultures and languages? Allow me to explain its relevance. When operating abroad, navigating through unfamiliar landscapes demands an unwavering commitment to trust. It acts as the thread that weaves together different cultural fabrics, fostering mutual understanding and camaraderie. Throughout my personal journey, I've realized that effective and frequent communication lies at the heart of building trust. Take the time to genuinely listen to your business partners, suppliers, staff and customers, and respond to their needs with timeliness and efficiency.

Addressing issues proactively is the key, for it prevents unnecessary escalations and nurtures a sense of dependability. Staying true to your word is equally paramount, as it instills confidence in your integrity and reliability. Transparency in business practices is yet another crucial aspect of cultivating trust. By openly and honestly sharing your goals, timelines, and financial expectations with partners and suppliers, you lay the groundwork for a trustworthy relationship free from potential conflicts and misunderstandings.

However, let us not overlook the human element of building trust. Build personal connections with your business partners, beyond the confines of a Zoom meeting. Invest time in getting to know them on both a professional and personal level. Engage in conversations about families, hobbies, and shared passions, like the love of food. Such interactions can create profound bonds that foster enduring trust and loyalty. A vivid memory comes to mind—one that exemplifies the power of building trust through personal connections. I vividly recall the day I met one of my key suppliers in Mexico. Despite months of email exchanges and video calls, it was our face-to-face meeting that transformed our relationship. We instantly connected on a personal level, sharing stories about our lives and our mutual love for the culinary arts. This personal bond served as the catalyst for a flourishing business partnership—one that eventually became instrumental in expanding my restaurant empire in Mexico.

Let this advice resonate deeply: trust is the cornerstone of success. Dedicate yourself to nurturing honest and meaningful relationships, communicating effectively and promptly, and adhering to the principles of transparency in your business practices. By doing so, you will undoubtedly pave the path towards building an enduring and thriving restaurant enterprise- one that not only delights the palates of your customers but also earns their unwavering trust for years to come.

Championship Team Mentality

As an entrepreneur in the restaurant industry, I've come to realize that the world of business and sports have more in common than you might think. Both require a combination of individual talent and teamwork to achieve success. And as the saying goes, "talent wins games, teamwork wins championships." But it's not just about having a team in place. It's about having the right people in the right roles, who are dedicated to the success of the organization. In other words, it's about human capital. Your employees are the backbone of your business, and building a strong and dedicated team is essential to achieving your goals. As a leader, it's your responsibility to create an environment where your employees can thrive, and where their interests align with the interests of the organization. In this chapter, we'll delve into the importance of human capital to an organization and how to build leadership from within by building trust. Once you build trust and loyalty within your team, you can create a culture of productivity and success.

I know firsthand the impact that a strong team can have on a business. When your employees are invested in the success of the organization, they are more motivated and productive. And when your leadership team is aligned with the goals of the business, you can achieve incredible results. You should aim to build a strong team, develop leadership from within, and create a culture of trust and loyalty. Because at the end of the day, it's not just about winning games, it's about winning championships. And that starts with building a winning team.

When it comes to achieving success in any industry, the power of teamwork cannot be underestimated. Throughout my years in the restaurant industry, I've come to realize that individual talent has its limits. In fact, relying solely on individual skill sets can lead to a fragmented team dynamic and even jeopardize the success of the business. That's why I made it my mission to create a "championship team" in my restaurant. To do so, I sought to build a team that was diverse in talent and experience, while also emphasizing the importance of working together towards a common goal. When everyone on the team is focused on accomplishing a common goal instead of individual successes, it creates a more positive and supportive work environment.

One of the most pervasive challenges in the restaurant industry is the existence of seemingly two separate teams within a single establishment: the front-of-house versus the back-of-house. This rivalry has become almost legendary. When everything is going well, these teams can function as best friends, but the moment something goes awry, the restaurant transforms into a battleground of finger-pointing, with the unfortunate customer caught in the crossfire. This is precisely why fostering a "championship mentality" becomes paramount. In the restaurant industry, it is crucial to prioritize teamwork and place the needs of the guests above all else. From the back-of-house team to the front-of-house team, everyone must work together to create an exceptional dining experience. This not only leads to better service but also fosters a sense of camaraderie and trust among team members. However, building this mentality is not always easy. In a fast-paced and high-stress environment like a restaurant, it can be challenging to maintain positivity and teamwork. But by prioritizing a supportive work environment and encouraging collaboration, a restaurant can achieve exceptional results and stand out in a highly competitive industry.

Building Leadership From Within

If you're looking to build a championship team within your organization, you'll need to focus on building trust amongst your players and one of the best ways to do this is by building leadership from within. When I first started, I knew that I needed to find the right people to help me build it from the ground up. As a leader faced with the challenges of managing limited resources and navigating uncharted territory in the realm of employment, I had to adopt a strategic approach to my hiring decisions. It was during this process that I came to deeply understand the significance of self-awareness, particularly when it came to building my winning team. This often overlooked yet crucial trait became the cornerstone of my decision-making process. Recognizing my own strengths, weaknesses, and leadership style became paramount. Through this introspective journey, I gained a profound understanding of the importance of seeking out individuals whose skill sets complemented mine. I realized that hiring decisions were far more than merely adding names to a roster; they represented pivotal investments in the future of my business. Guided by self-awareness, I looked beyond conventional qualifications and experience levels. While experience certainly held merit, I sought individuals who not only displayed talent but also showed the potential to learn and grow with the team.

That's when I met my diamond in the rough. She was a twenty-six year-old who walked into my office interviewing for the Operations Manager position. At first glance, it seemed like this young and ambitious woman was trying to bite more than she could chew. Nonetheless, even after having already interviewed over fifty candidates earlier that week that had failed to meet my expectations, I decided to sit down with her and give her a tough interview. In my mind, at the very least she would gain valuable interviewing experience at her young age. To my surprise, while she lacked empirical experience, her energy and drive stood out to me. She was confident in her industry knowledge but grounded and humble. She was ambitious in her career goals but willing to work hard for them and methodical in her approach. I immediately liked her. Although her experience was limited, you can tell a lot about a person with how they deal with hardship and approach challenges in their lives. There was something about her that seemed right. I think what drew me more to her was that she complimented my leadership style. I decided to take a chance on her and explore her untapped potential. I pushed her hard since day one and she always had the best attitude, always eager to learn, worked harder than anyone, and was continuously looking for ways to improve the business. She quickly became an integral part of our team and proved her worth time and time again. As our business grew, so did her role in the organization. She took on more responsibilities and ultimately became a key player in our operations department. Despite her relative lack of experience, she was always looking for ways to streamline our processes and make our team more efficient. Her hard work and dedication paid off, and she eventually became the Director of Operations and my most trusted employee. She had earned the respect and admiration of the entire team through her commitment, passion, and work ethic.

My advice is simple, get to know yourself and be honest about your areas of opportunity for growth. Manage those shortcomings by building a winning team around you. Look beyond conventional credentials and experience, true talent is not just something you can see on a piece of paper in black an white, it's someone's values, their mentality and their passion.

Once you have found your diamond, nurture it. By investing in this particular employee and providing her with opportunities to grow and develop within our organization, we forged a team that exuded loyalty, commitment, and passion for our shared goals. By actively seeking out and investing in talented individuals already within your organization, you can cultivate a team of strong leaders dedicated to your company's success. It is crucial to identify the diamonds in the rough and invest in the right people. While investing in talent may demand careful consideration and effort, it is undeniably profitable in the long run. These invested individuals not only bring exceptional skills and expertise to the table, but they also become ambassadors of your organization's values and vision. They are more likely to stay loyal, committed, and motivated, leading to reduced turnover and recruitment costs. Additionally, a leadership team that has been nurtured from within carries a deep understanding of your company's culture, ensuring consistency and coherence in your operations.

Identifying and nurturing leadership within a restaurant organization can undoubtedly be an arduous task, given the numerous challenges in the industry. The high turnover rate, which is common in restaurants, makes it challenging to retain skilled individuals who could otherwise contribute significantly to the business's growth. Furthermore, limited resources for talent development and the absence of structured talent management programs impede the establishment of clear career paths and growth opportunities for ambitious employees, especially for smaller establishments. Also, in such a highly competitive hiring environment, smaller restaurants may find it challenging to attract and retain top talent compared to larger chains or well-established establishments. Moreover, the fast-paced nature of the restaurant industry poses communication and feedback challenges, which are crucial for effectively nurturing talent. The intense operational demands of running a restaurant leave little time for owners to focus on talent development, as they must juggle customer service, kitchen management, and administrative tasks. That's why I've developed some creative techniques to spot raw talent and build a culture with a championship mentality.

Hiring your Team

To be able to recognize diamonds in the rough, you first need a team that possesses the right talent. And what does that mean? It means finding a group of individuals who have the necessary skills, knowledge, and attitude to excel in their roles. They should be customer-oriented, team players, and passionate about their jobs. While this may sound generic, the truth is that every restaurant has its own unique needs and characteristics. Therefore, there is no one-size-fits-all answer, but you must analyze all these traits to know you are on the right path.

I can hear some of my fellow restaurateurs arguing with me about this, frustrated by how hard it is to attract talent, period. Well, I agree. Finding good talent in this industry sometimes seems impossible due to various reasons: high turnover rates, demanding work environments with long hours and high stress, and the perception of limited job stability. Moreover, many employees view restaurant jobs as temporary or part-time positions, making it challenging to attract skilled individuals. However, it is not impossible, and it all starts with recruitment.

One of the most powerful tools I've discovered for successful recruitment is filtering. You have to weed out the candidates that are not ideal. Obviously, it depends on the position, but in my opinion, I would rather have a candidate with no experience but has the best attitude, than a seasoned "know it all". You can't teach passion, good vibes, and work ethic. To recruit the best talent, the first filter is your job post. Similar to dating, attracting the right person depends on your profile, in this case your job post description. Words and context matter significantly. Make sure you are specific and give the candidate a feel for the role and the work environment and most importantly who your company is. Remember, you are both choosing each other.

Let me give you an example of why and how we started attracting the right talent. We were consistently getting one-star reviews because of poor service, so we established a series of weekly training sessions for our Front of the House staff.

Although the service improved, we realized the problem was not the lack of knowledge but our team. Although most of my staff were experienced, and I would say they were good sellers, something was missing. They weren't meeting the expectations of our customers, and despite having a fairly low turnover rate, it wasn't translating into strong customer rapport. So, I brainstormed with my team and we analyzed the possible reasons behind it. What were we missing? The results showed that there was nothing inherently wrong with our waiters, but their mindset and motivators weren't aligned with what we were trying to accomplish. Therefore, we needed to make bigger changes, so we decided to change the job name and description and began recruiting for hosts instead of waiters. We created a tailored job description and began filtering candidates based on aptitude. We made sure to interview only those candidates who scored highly proficient in customer service. Most importantly, we started looking for people whose mindsets and motivators aligned with who we were as a company.

To identify these traits, candidates were given a forty-five-minute evaluation questionnaire even before the interview process. This questionnaire provided an assessment of a candidate's skills, motivators, personality traits, and core values. These traits were useful in determining if a candidate was a good fit for the specific job and company culture. It also helped us identify the potential job performance based on a candidate's cognitive abilities, problem-solving skills, and work ethic. This was particularly useful for management positions that require critical thinking or complex decision-making. This method of filtering candidates proved to be the most effective one we have ever utilized. It allowed us to focus on the core competencies that were essential for our business, without wasting time and resources on the wrong candidates. So don't be afraid of filtering and use these techniques to find the right players for your team. Remember this process may seem long and tedious but you are building your championship team for the long-term.

After filtering candidates based on the evaluation, your next and most important filter is the actual interview. A physical interview provides the opportunity for face-to-face interaction, which can help you assess the candidate's interpersonal skills, communication style, and overall presence. It also allows the candidate to get a sense of the company culture and work environment. In addition to verbal communication, physical interviews allow you to observe non-verbal cues, such as body language and facial expressions. If properly analyzed, these cues can provide valuable insights into a candidate's confidence level, sincerity, and interest in the job. One-on-one interviews also provide a platform for you to ask in-depth questions or clarifications about a candidate's experience and qualifications. This can help to clarify any ambiguity in the candidate's resume or evaluation and provide a more comprehensive understanding of who they are.

The final two aspects of a physical interview that are usually overlooked are showcasing the company culture and establishing the human connection.

Physical interviews provide the opportunity for you to showcase your company culture and values. This can help to attract candidates who align with the company's mission and vision, and create a more positive impression of the company. As stated earlier you are both choosing each other. I believe in reciprocity and understand that quality candidates are also interviewing the companies they want to work for.

Using the dating analogy again, think of these interviews as a first date. Give them the time and space needed to allow for a genuine human connection to be established between you and the candidate. This connection helps to build trust and rapport, which is important for a successful working relationship and the foundation for building the championship mentality amongst your team.

As you can imagine, we didn't always have this comprehensive process for hiring personnel. As my organization grew, I found myself struggling to keep up with the increasing demand for qualified personnel. With more people involved during the hiring process, transferring my intuition, criteria and knowledge became unrealistic and I had to find a sustainable solution. Of course we made some mistakes along the way, hiring individuals who were not a good fit for our team. But we didn't let those mistakes stop us from finding the right people. We recognized the need for a systematic approach to ensure that we recruited the best team players, regardless of who was leading the process. That's how this evaluation and filtering process came into being. It was the result of our trial and error, and a crucial part of our adaptation process as we expanded our business. Though it was painful, let me tell you, it was definitely worth it. It helped me build a team of passionate, skilled and dedicated individuals who have contributed to the success of my restaurant business. So, if you are struggling with your recruiting process, I encourage you to try this method. With the right people on your team, you can achieve anything you set your mind to.

Team Development

Unfortunately, recruiting a talented team is only half the battle. The real challenge lies in keeping them engaged and invested in the success of the business. One effective way to achieve this is by understanding and recognizing your employees' motivators. Motivation and employee engagement are closely interconnected. When employees are motivated, they are more likely to align their personal goals with those of your business. When their aspirations and values resonate with the company's mission, they become more engaged in actively contributing to the organization's success.

When I first started my business, I had a small team of servers and cooks. As we grew, I began to notice one of my cooks who had a natural ability to lead and motivate his teammates. However, he was also a troublemaker who liked to challenge authority and make waves. Instead of giving up on him, I decided to invest in his development and offer him a leadership position within the organization. I wanted to build trust with him and thought of aligning his interests with those of the organization, by offering him a role that leveraged his natural leadership skills. I made him the lead of the kitchen staff, responsible for overseeing the daily tasks of the team. It wasn't an easy decision, but I felt confident that it was the right one. I was taking a chance on someone who had shown me that he was capable of great things, even if he had a bit of a rebellious streak. And it paid off. He not only became a great manager but also one of my most loyal allies in the organization. By investing in him, I showed him that I believed in his abilities, and I gave him a chance to prove himself. I also demonstrated that I was committed to his success and wanted to help him reach his full potential. Another effective way to build trust with your team is by keeping them motivated by promoting development and growth. By offering development opportunities, you demonstrate that you recognize the potential and talent of your employees and are invested in their future. This creates a positive work environment and a motivated team that is eager to contribute to the company's success and one that remains engaged for the long term. I personally learned this organically. I can honestly say that at the beginning of my journey, it wasn't even a purposeful action. Let me get a little personal and explain. Developing this US brand in Mexico was so much more than just a business opportunity for me. Coming from an immigrant background, I have lived and learned how the simple act of giving people opportunities, resources, and genuine support to become better can radically transform their lives. With this new business venture, I had the opportunity to do just that and bring that ethos back to Mexico. In the beginning, most of my employees were skeptical about my motives behind this new and uncommon leadership style, as it was seen as highly unorthodox behavior in a place like Mexico City. But as time went by, they began embracing it, then appreciating it, and soon enough amazing things began to happen.

When you're not recruiting talent you should be developing it. As I once read, the only thing worse than losing a team member after having trained them is keeping them on your team untrained.

I was always on the lookout for raw talent within my organization. Whether it was a server with a knack for customer service or a dishwasher who was an expert at multitasking, I made sure to recognize and reward their efforts. I would offer them opportunities to learn new skills, take on new responsibilities, and advance in their careers. It is important to remember that your employees are the backbone of your business. Without them, your dreams and ambitions would not be possible. Therefore, it is crucial to invest in your employees' development, which includes not just their professional but personal as well. In my experience, investing in personal development can take many forms. It could mean providing opportunities for your employees to attend conferences, workshops, and training sessions outside of their normal job duties. For me it means personally coaching them to support their overall well-being. I take personal development seriously. I become invested in the personal success of my team members. By helping your employees grow as individuals, you are also helping them develop new skills that can benefit your business. For example, an employee who learns how to manage their time effectively or communicate more clearly can bring those skills back to their role in your organization. This can lead to improved performance, increased productivity, and better outcomes for your business. Of course, investing in personal development requires a financial investment or in my case a time commitment. However, the benefits far outweigh the costs. My team was more engaged, more committed, and more invested in the success of the business. They knew that I believed in them and that I was willing to invest in their futures.

That's how you build a winning team- by recognizing talent, nurturing it, and aligning it with the goals of the organization.

Let me tell you about one of the employees I'm most proud of. He started with us as a cook in our restaurant, but he quickly caught my eye with his strong work ethic and commitment. We promoted him to kitchen lead, where he continued to take on more responsibilities and continuously go above and beyond. But there was one problem- he was a perfectionist who would often just do tasks himself if he felt his team wasn't doing them up to his standards. Instead of letting this continue, I saw it as an opportunity for him to develop his leadership and communication skills. We worked on delegating effectively and communicating with his team, even going so far as to have him work in the kitchen without the use of his hands to force him to rely on his team and communicate with them. And it paid off - before long, he became the assistant kitchen manager of our flagship location. This promotion boosted his confidence and he soon started looking for ways to continue growing and learning. He decided to enter culinary school to acquire the theoretical and administrative side of his passion. He completed his whole course while working for us, and I was excited and supportive of his decision. I offered him a flexible schedule, homework hours during his shift and other benefits to help him through this new challenge. Once again it paid off. After finishing school he showed interest and aptitude in the administrative side of the business, and we eventually promoted him to corporate chef. As our corporate chef, he developed innovative and delicious new dishes and demonstrated excellent leadership skills by mentoring and training our cooks and kitchen managers. He helped streamline our kitchen processes ensuring efficient cost control management. The story doesn't end there - he continued to grow and excel, eventually being promoted to operations manager where he oversaw the day-to-day operations of our restaurant. His journey from cook to operations manager is a shining example of the power of developing your team. By investing in both his personal and professional growth we fostered a loyal and dedicated employee who was committed to our organization's success.

The Power of Transparency

When you prioritize open and honest communication, you foster a positive work environment where employees feel valued, included, and well-informed. This sense of belonging creates a strong emotional connection to the company, leading to increased loyalty and commitment. By genuinely sharing the company's vision, mission, and goals with your employees, they can understand how their work directly contributes to the overall success of the business.

I learned the power of transparency firsthand when I struggled to get my employees to understand the importance of cost control. By sharing financial reports with my kitchen team and explaining how different expenses affected our bottom line, my employees were able to understand the impact of their actions and become more engaged and motivated. This increased transparency ultimately led to a more productive and invested team. Employees trust leaders who are willing to share information openly, even during challenging times. By communicating openly, I witnessed a remarkable shift in my team's mindset, turning challenges into opportunities and fostering a culture of accountability and dedication.

As we conclude this chapter, I would like to reiterate my advice from earlier: build trust. As it pertains to your team, there is no better way to keep them engaged and motivated than by building trust. Build trust and their loyalty and commitment will follow. Building trust within an organization is not easy, and it requires authenticity, empathy, and a commitment to leading by example. Through personal experience, I have learned that effective leadership means creating a culture of openness, collaboration, and mutual respect, where all employees feel valued and are encouraged to share their thoughts and ideas.

As a leader, you must be willing to roll up your sleeves and demonstrate the behavior you expect from your employees. Celebrate exceptional performance, recognize good work, and foster a positive workplace culture that values teamwork and community. By doing so, you can create a culture of trust and loyalty that leads to improved morale, increased productivity, and greater employee retention.

Your team is the backbone of your business, and it is your job as their leader to develop their skills and create a championship mentality that leads them to victory. I can assure you that if you focus on building trust, you can build a strong and unified organization that is aligned around a common vision and values. So take the lessons from this book and apply them to your own leadership journey. Your team, and your business, will thank you for it.

Chapter 4:

The Heartbeat of Success

Organizational culture is an intangible yet influential force that shapes every aspect of a company. It establishes the tone for employee interactions, decision-making processes, and overall work dynamics. Possessing a healthy and positive organizational culture is a vital asset for ensuring the success of your business. However, building a strong and positive company culture is not only a complex task but also an ongoing journey. It demands dedication, adaptability, and a sincere desire to cultivate a work environment where employees feel valued, engaged, and connected to the company's values and mission. In simple words, it is crucial that employees genuinely love the company they work for. This chapter will explore the importance of cultivating employee love for a company and how it can drive a strong organizational culture.

When I first started my journey, I used to believe that creating a positive organizational culture was a daunting task that required a significant investment of time, money, and energy. To me, it seemed like a futile effort that did not yield any measurable results. Being a data-driven person, I used to think that the return on investment of building a positive organizational culture was intangible and difficult to quantify. I thought that it would distract my business from its primary objectives, such as generating revenue, profits, and growth. I also believed that creating a positive organizational culture was a fleeting endeavor that could quickly deteriorate if not continuously monitored and reinforced. It seemed like a never-ending cycle that would consume my time and resources. To be completely honest, I was skeptical about the benefits of investing in organizational culture.

However, as I gained more experience as a business owner, I realized that I was wrong. It quickly became obvious to me why organizational culture is the very foundation upon which businesses thrive and prosper. Especially within an industry where the customer experience is paramount, cultivating a positive culture has immediate impacts on employees, customers, and the overall financial picture. Looking back, I wish it hadn't taken me two years into my journey to realize this. The development of a positive organizational culture wasn't just important- it turned out to be an absolute necessity for success. Let me explain why.

Have you ever wondered what sets apart a remarkable restaurant experience from a mediocre one? One secret ingredient that can make all the difference is your organizational culture. In an industry built on human interactions, customers can quickly pick up on the vibe of a restaurant, and that can make or break their dining experience. And here's a revelation: "that vibe" is none other than your organizational culture.

Organizational culture is more than just a buzzword- it's the unique set of beliefs, values, norms, behaviors, and practices that shape the overall work environment and interactions within your company and influence how your employees behave. It is like the collective personality of an organization, influencing how employees and leaders conduct themselves, make decisions, and work together. Moreover, organizational culture plays a crucial role in shaping employee love for a company, and believe me, employees' love matters.

Employees must love your company before your customers do.

As a business owner, it's easy to get lost in the day-to-day operations of the company and overlook the most vital asset- your employees. However, it is imperative to understand that your employees are the ones who interact with your customers every day, and they shape their experience with your brand. That's why it's crucial to cultivate employee love for your company. When employees genuinely love their company, they become highly engaged, motivated, and deeply committed to their work. They take ownership of their roles and proudly become brand ambassadors. Their loyalty to the company strengthens, making them less likely to seek opportunities elsewhere. Moreover, they enthusiastically share positive experiences with others, resulting in increased brand awareness and a positive reputation. It's a win-win situation: when your employees are happy, your customers are more likely to be happy too. When employees develop a strong connection and affinity towards their company, it serves as a clear indication that the company has effectively nurtured a positive and supportive culture.

On the other hand, a negative or unhealthy organizational culture can lead to a wide range of consequences that can significantly impact the company's performance, employee well-being, and overall success. A negative company culture is closely linked to a toxic work environment and can cause employees to feel dissatisfied, disengaged, and unmotivated. This, in turn, leads to frustration, stress, and the development of resentment and cynicism towards management, along with a lack of loyalty and eventual burnout. As a result, your company will experience high employee turnover, reduced productivity, and difficulty attracting top talent. The negative environment can also have a ripple effect on the company's brand image and may result in poor customer service.

Five Essential Principles

This is why, as a leader, one must prioritize the creation of a positive organizational culture that fosters employees' love for the company, and it all starts with you. As the driving force behind your company's vision, values, and strategic direction, you play a crucial role in shaping a strong and positive culture and work environment. Although let's be honest, this is easier said than done. So, how can you go about creating a positive organizational culture that your employees love? Is it as easy as grabbing a quick template from the internet and applying it to your business? Well, let me tell you, unfortunately, it's not that simple. There's no one-size-fits-all template that fits all scenarios; it's a concept that needs to be customized according to your company's unique goals and requirements. However, here are 5 foundational principles that can provide you with the essential elements to build such a culture:

1. Define your Values: As a leader, defining values involves pinpointing the fundamental principles that steer your organization's operations. These values need to be linked with your overarching goals, forming clear statements that outline how you want

your team to conduct themselves and collaborate. If your business is already established, the initial step is understanding your organization's present culture. Even if it might not be explicitly stated, every company possesses an organizational culture that subtly influences processes and interactions. It's like an invisible thread interwoven into daily choices and actions. Recognizing this culture is essential because it forms the foundation on which your company operates. By comprehending the existing culture, you can better align your decisions. Defining values then becomes a conscious tool to shape and direct this pre-existing culture. Once these values are outlined, ensuring every member of your organization grasps them becomes paramount. This lays the foundation for fostering a positive and vibrant work environment.

2. Lead by Example: As a leader, it's vital to exemplify the behavior you wish to see in your employees. When leaders actively practice the behaviors, values, and attitudes they expect from

their team, they wield a potent influence that permeates the entire workplace. This consistent showcase of integrity, dedication, communication, and collaboration not only cultivates trust and credibility among employees but also molds a culture where these traits become the standard. By embodying these qualities, leaders motivate their team members to follow suit, resulting in heightened motivation, increased productivity, enhanced communication, and a shared dedication to the organization's triumph. Treating your employees with respect, expressing gratitude for their hard work, and fostering a positive work environment are all part of this process.

3. Promote Collaboration: Encourage your employees to collaborate and provide mutual support. Teamwork and collaboration play a pivotal role in shaping a positive organizational culture. When individuals join forces as a team, they share a common purpose and hold each other's contributions in high regard. This nurtures trust,

facilitates effective communication, and sparks innovation. Collaborative settings foster not only learning and problem-solving but also the cultivation of robust relationships among team members, resulting in elevated employee engagement and heightened productivity. Through collaborative efforts, employees can tackle challenges, harness their distinct skills, and collectively achieve shared objectives, ultimately forging a harmonious and thriving workplace. This dynamic fosters a sense of community and contributes to a positive work environment.

4. Acknowledge and Incentivize: Acknowledge and reward outstanding efforts. Take the time to celebrate the achievements of your employees and offer incentives for exceptional performance. When your team's hard work is acknowledged and rewarded, it nurtures a sense of engagement, motivation, and significance in the workplace. This recognition sets in motion a positive cycle of heightened dedication and performance, fostering a

healthy spirit of competition and skills enhancement while reinforcing the organization's core values. A combination of acknowledgment from both peers and leadership, along with clear criteria for incentives, creates an atmosphere where collaboration, morale, and loyalty flourish. In the long run, these practices contribute to a culture where employees feel empowered, inspired to excel, and honored for their contributions. This, in turn, cultivates a more productive and gratifying work environment. Examples of such recognition can encompass bonuses, promotions and public acclaim.

5. Embrace Feedback: Welcoming feedback as a leader is essential in cultivating a positive organizational culture. When leaders proactively seek and cherish input from their team, it fosters trust, open communication, and a feeling of empowerment. Make it a habit to frequently solicit feedback from your employees and take meaningful actions based on it. This sends a clear message that their perspectives are highly regarded and their

contributions can catalyze positive transformations within the organization. This practice promotes a continuous loop of learning, problem-solving, and innovation throughout the company. Leaders play a key role in nurturing an environment where employees feel engaged, appreciated, and motivated to bring their best to the table. Ultimately, this contributes to a collaborative and flourishing workplace atmosphere.

I can completely understand if, after going through all of this information, you feel overwhelmed, like your owner's to-do list just went from challenging to impossible. But it's important you don't perceive it that way.

Crafting a positive culture takes time and unwavering commitment, but believe me when I say the effort is well worth it.

As a fellow business owner, I can assure you that establishing a positive organizational culture isn't something that can be achieved overnight. It's a process that requires continuous effort and reinforcement. So, it's really crucial for you to explore various avenues until you uncover the opportunities and strategies that naturally weave these essential aspects into your continuous growth process. Instead of thinking of your organizational culture as something task-oriented, consider it an ever-evolving work in progress. These opportunities to cultivate this culture can arise in various manners and at any point during your journey. That's why I'd like to share a few personal strategies that have worked effectively for me. These examples should give you valuable insights into how you can approach this mission in your own journey.

Self-Empowerment

As you can probably guess from my confession, I used to believe that building a positive culture was a time-consuming and costly endeavor, consequently, my business wasn't always characterized by such a culture. Unfortunately, this led to a cycle of high employee turnover, diminished morale, and poor customer service. It was only when I recognized that these issues were rooted in my organizational culture that I actively decided to undertake the task of crafting a culture that my employees could genuinely love and thrive within. And it all kicked off with a straightforward yet impactful move: empowerment.

I empowered my employees with the autonomy to make decisions and take ownership and accountability for their work. This cultivated a profound sense of pride and ownership among the staff, resulting in elevated customer service and heightened employee morale. One particular instance that stands out is the launch of our monthly special. Similar to many fellow culinary enthusiasts, my kitchen manager possessed an abundance of creativity and passion. While he fully recognized the importance of adhering to our standardized recipes and processes, the day-to-day constraints were stifling his enthusiasm and becoming a hindrance. He frequently presented daring concepts for new dishes he wished to introduce to the menu, and my typical response was a decisive "NO." I was acutely aware of the potential challenges and costs that even a single new item could bring about, and I was not prepared to take uncalculated risks solely for his satisfaction. However, upon further exploration, I began to uncover the underlying motivations driving his proposals. This prompted me to consider a different approach, one that was both systematic and strategic. I extended an opportunity for collaboration on a monthly special featuring our main dish. I stipulated specific guidelines encompassing costs, processes, and timeframes he needed to adhere to. In addition to creating the dish, he assumed responsibility for the necessary training hours and designing the structures that would ensure consistent product quality. The special was unveiled at the beginning of each month, followed by a thorough evaluation. I also emphasized that given the requisite marketing investment, this initiative constituted a one-year commitment. After comprehensive discussions, we collectively agreed to the terms, and the outcomes stemming from this venture were nothing short of remarkable. Not only did my restaurant witness a surge in business, but this monthly special also garnered favor among both our front-of-house and back-of-house teams. The impact on our organizational culture proved to be invaluable, and the sustained rise in sales served as a testament to its effectiveness.

Respect and Mutual Support

Another strategic approach I adopted centered around cultivating a culture deeply grounded in respect and mutual support. I encouraged employees to collaborate and stand by each other, fostering a sense of camaraderie and collective endeavor. Recognizing that the foundation of this culture had to originate from my role as the leader, that's precisely where I set it in motion. I initiated individual discussions with each of my teams, delving into their challenges while clearly articulating my expectations. Simultaneously, I encouraged them to share their perspectives on aspects they believed required enhancements within their respective roles. These conversations organically evolved into both team-oriented and individual challenges. In these scenarios, I personally undertook the challenges to demonstrate to my staff that the objectives I set were not just attainable, but also intended to push their boundaries. By embarking on these challenges, I gained an unfiltered view of the actual hurdles they faced. This unique insight empowered me to make well-informed decisions that not only optimized our operations but also served as an added advantage. I must admit, the moment my employees caught wind of my involvement in the challenges, their engagement levels soared. Imagine the motivation they derived from either trying to prove me wrong or merely wanting to compete with me. I immersed myself in various roles, from being a server or bartender for a day to working as a pizza cook and handling prep tasks- I embraced them all. What added an amusing twist was how team members in the same positions came together during these challenges, aiming to outperform me. Gradually and almost organically, these teams morphed into a unified front. This strategy not only elevated communication and productivity but also transformed our restaurant into a more fulfilling and enjoyable workplace.

Rising Stars

One of the strategies that truly hit the mark in cultivating a positive organizational culture involved spotlighting our "rising stars" as exemplars for the entire team. A "rising star" was an employee who had demonstrated exceptional talent and potential for growth within the organization. They might have begun in an entry-level role, yet through their hard work and dedication, they grew through the ranks to become a key player in the company.

By shining a spotlight on these rising stars and using them as role models for the rest of the team, we fostered a culture of excellence and inspired others to trailblaze their own paths of success.

Throughout my journey, I encountered a considerable number of "rising stars". However, among them, there was one standout who not only made a lasting impression but also became an icon within my company. Among my staff, there was one employee who had been with our restaurant since the beginning. He started as a delivery driver, but it quickly became clear that he was meant for much more than his role, he was talented with numbers, he was committed and driven to learning and growth. As this realization dawned on me, my desire extended beyond retaining him on the team; I was genuinely motivated to facilitate his advancement within the organization. Over the next few years, he worked his way up the ranks. He became the head of delivery drivers, a cashier, a key employee, then an assistant general manager, and eventually the general manager of our flagship location. His leadership skills, work ethic and dedication to the job were unparalleled. He was always willing to go above and beyond for the company, the customers and the team. He became a role model for other employees, showing them what was possible with hard work and dedication. But it wasn't just his success that made him a poster boy for our organization. It was his attitude and approach to the job. He genuinely loved the company and its values, and he always went out of his way to make sure that other employees felt the same way. He was a true ambassador for our organizational culture.

The concept of "rising stars" in my company extended beyond promotions; it encompassed recognizing employees for their achievements, growth, and alignment with our core values.

Drawing from my background as an ex-athlete, with the sports culture deeply ingrained in me, I introduced a similar award system at our annual end-of-year celebration. Each time a rising star achieved something remarkable, I ensured that their accomplishments were celebrated. This not only demonstrated our gratitude for their efforts but also sent a clear message to the entire team: commitment and hard work were genuinely recognized and esteemed within our organization. As our rising stars continued to thrive, we extended mentorship and guidance to them. This approach not only nurtured their individual development but also established a precedent that underscored the accessibility of mentorship and support for anyone with aspirations of excelling.

These rising stars became examples of success, fostering a culture of excellence where employees were spurred to put in more effort and strive for their own achievements. By showcasing their accomplishments, we demonstrated to the entire team what could be accomplished and inspired them to pursue their own aspirations.

Your employees are the backbone of your business, and their satisfaction has a direct impact on your business profitability. Take the time to actively listen to your employees, demonstrate the value you place on their contributions, and offer avenues for their growth and advancement. Embrace achievements and take accountability for missteps. Cultivate transparency and maintain consistent communication with your team. Create an environment where they feel like an integral part of the family.

The key takeaway: don't hesitate to invest in cultivating a positive organizational culture. Allocating your time, finances, and resources to building a strong culture can pay off significantly in the long term.

Indeed, creating a positive organizational culture demands a comprehensive approach, an ongoing effort that should be integrated into every aspect of your business, even though it may seem like a challenge. But, drawing from my own experience, I can tell you firsthand that the investment in fostering a positive organizational culture is not just rewarding, it is imperative to your business's success.

In the previous chapters, we've been delving into what I often refer to as the "essence" of your business. I use the term "essence" because it encapsulates that inner drive, fervor, and distinctive character that truly defines your business. Just as each individual possesses a unique essence, a restaurant's essence mirrors both the owner's identity and the combined spirit of its staff. However, let's be practical- as enchanting as this concept is, much like humans, essences require a tangible form to exist. In our case, that's the tangible business itself.

We are not looking for our restaurants to not merely survive, we are looking for them to truly flourish. With this in mind, our business' physical health, particularly its financial stability, must be rock-solid. It should be robust enough not only to keep the business afloat but also to fuel its expansion. That's why the upcoming chapters will delve deep into the intricacies of how you can nurture and optimize this pivotal facet. Once you've aligned these two elements in seamless harmony, there's just one final elusive element left to unveil- the one that holds the master key to your ultimate recipe for success.

Chapter 5 :

The Secret Sauce

You and I share a common pursuit- the quest for success in an industry that's both exhilarating and demanding. We can all agree that revenue is the lifeblood of our business, and without it, we wouldn't have a business at all, but there's a secret sauce that's even more potent: our profit. If you think about it, profit is the true measure of your success- it's what's left in your pocket after every expense is taken care of. So, while having a high revenue is fantastic, if your profit isn't stacking up, it's time to shift your focus. So, if profit is the secret sauce, here's the two ingredients necessary to boost the flavor: tracking productivity and managing expenses. In this chapter, I'll show why embracing productivity is the game-changer for your restaurant's success. Let's roll up our sleeves and uncover how to harness the power of productivity metrics to amplify profits.

At the heart of our industry lies the balance between passion and profit. We all understand the exhilaration of seeing revenue flowing in, but maybe we've been focusing on the wrong number. Your profit isn't just a number; it's a reflection of your business's health after all costs are settled. It's what enables growth, innovation, and sustainability. So today, I'm taking you on a journey to explore how focusing on productivity metrics can be the key to not only boosting your revenue but also supercharging your profit.

Tracking Productivity

Let's kick things off by diving into the realm of labor costs. As restaurant owners, we know that labor costs can be one of our most significant expenses. Imagine having the ability to fine-tune these costs to align perfectly with customer demand- that's where the magic of tracking productivity metrics comes into play. By analyzing metrics like tables turned per hour or dishes prepared per hour, you can strike that delicate balance between staffing levels and customer flow. The result? Reduced labor costs without compromising the quality of your service. Think of productivity metrics as your backstage pass to labor efficiency- the key to turning a full house into a full pocket. But how do we put this theory into practice? Let's get practical. Embrace the analysis of technology like time clocks or scheduling software. These tools give your management team the ability to analyze your team's productivity during their shifts. It's like having a behind-the-scenes peek at your kitchen's performance. When you see who's shining and who might need a helping hand, you can take action to elevate the whole team's performance.

Tracking productivity will support your team's growth. If you're not analyzing your data and leveraging technology, what's the point? Have you ever encountered an employee who seems to be lagging behind? Rather than turning a blind eye, consider this an opportunity to mentor and develop. By tapping into productivity metrics, you can pinpoint areas where additional training or resources can make a significant impact. I've seen it firsthand- a little guidance can turn an underperformer into a true asset. It's a win-win, boosting your team's morale and your bottom line simultaneously. For me, tracking productivity metrics isn't just about data, but about igniting a transformation that still echoes in the walls of my business.

I once noticed a good server in my team who always seemed to be a step behind in the efficiency race. Instead of brushing it off or simply hoping for improvement, I decided to dive headfirst into the issue. You see, this was more than just about numbers- it was about nurturing a sense of collective growth and empowering my team. So, alongside my trusted team members, we embarked on a mission to dissect our operations and understand why. We didn't just analyze, we lived and breathed every step of the process. And what we uncovered were a series of operational bottlenecks that were holding us back. It was like peeling back layers to reveal the true heart of the matter. It wasn't just about identifying the problems, it was about finding creative solutions that aligned with the spirit of our restaurant. We recognized that some tasks could be automated to give our servers more time to engage with customers. We revamped our order processing system, introduced digital tools to streamline communication, and optimized our table-turnover process. The result? It wasn't just an uptick in efficiency – there was an entirely new vibrant energy running through the team. As the changes took shape, I saw the server who had been struggling step up, their confidence rising with each successful task completed. It wasn't just about the tasks; it was about empowering them to contribute in meaningful ways. But here's where the story takes a beautiful twist. It wasn't just that particular server who flourished. It was the entire team. The changes we implemented had a ripple effect, fostering a culture of collaboration and growth. Suddenly, the kitchen staff was working in tandem with the servers, and the front-of-house was in sync with the back-of-house. It was like the entire team was infused with a renewed sense of purpose. And that's the essence of this anecdote- the power of diving into the operational intricacies and finding solutions that resonate with your restaurant's soul. It's not just about the mechanics; it's about the heart you put into it. We didn't just optimize processes; we optimized our collective spirit.

Another benefit of focusing on productivity numbers is the ability to improve supply chain efficiency. By tracking inventory turnover and analyzing productivity numbers related to food preparation and cooking times, you can identify areas where supply chain efficiency can be improved. This can help reduce waste, minimize inventory costs, and ensure that the restaurant always has the right amount of ingredients on hand. Tracking productivity numbers can also help you streamline operations and reduce bottlenecks in the restaurant. By identifying areas where processes can be improved and optimizing kitchen layouts and cooking procedures, you can increase efficiency and reduce wait times. This can improve customer satisfaction and drive repeat business.

Imagine you're running your busy restaurant, where every minute counts and there's always something that needs to be done. You and your team are working tirelessly to provide excellent service to your customers, but sometimes it feels like you're just spinning your wheels. That's where tracking productivity numbers comes in. At first, we started tracking productivity just to keep ourselves accountable and see where we could improve. But we quickly realized that by doing so we were creating a culture of resourcefulness and accountability throughout the entire restaurant. By involving our staff in the tracking and analysis of productivity metrics, we were able to identify areas for improvement, work together to implement changes, and increase efficiency across the board. And the results were nothing short of amazing. Our staff was able to streamline their tasks, eliminate unnecessary steps, and find new ways to work smarter, not harder. What started as an internal drive for improvement soon transformed into a cultural shift. Our team was engaged, inspired, and eager to make strides together. Through brainstorming sessions and collaborative tweaks, we found ingenious ways to streamline operations. Our kitchen ran like a well-oiled machine, service was quicker, and smiles were abundant- from customers and staff alike.

But the real magic lies in how these productivity metrics can enhance the customer experience. Picture this: a bustling evening at my restaurant, every table filled with eager diners. Amidst the delightful chaos, there's a common challenge that we all face – wait times. It's a concern that resonates with every restaurateur, and it's where productivity metrics came to our rescue in a truly remarkable way. You see, it's not just about revenue numbers; it's about the customer experience. We decided to take the bull by the horns and use productivity metrics to dissect the wait time issue. It was like shining a spotlight on a problem that had been lurking in the shadows for too long. By analyzing the metrics related to table turnover, order processing times, and kitchen prep, we could pinpoint where the bottlenecks were occurring. We noticed that the wait times during peak hours were stretching uncomfortably. It wasn't just about the minutes ticking by and our inability to turn tables quickly; it was about the potential to dampen our guests' experience. That's when we turned to our treasure trove of customer feedback – a goldmine of insights waiting to be explored. We realized that our diners were patient, but time is of the essence, especially when they're ravenous. Armed with this insight, we decided to adjust our menu slightly. We introduced a selection of quick, delectable apps that our kitchen could whip up in a few minutes. The beauty was that these tweaks weren't just about speed; they were about crafting an even more delightful dining journey. And the results? Not only did we achieve reduced wait times we were delivering an experience that resonated with our patrons. Those quick appetizers not only satisfied their hunger but also showcased our commitment to providing a seamless experience. It was a tangible way of showing that we value their time just as much as they do. This experience showed me that if you focus on your guest's dining experience, the revenue will follow. It's about going beyond the surface and diving into the depths of your restaurant's operations.

By deciphering the metrics and blending them with the gems hidden within your customer feedback, you have the power to craft an unforgettable journey that can also impact your bottom line.

Remember, it's not just about boosting profit- it's about creating a symphony of flavors, efficiency, and impeccable service that resonates in every bite and every moment your guests spend at your restaurant. And when you succeed in doing that, you're not just building a loyal customer base; you're creating memories that will be talked about long after the plates are cleared.

Leverage Technology

As a restaurant owner, tracking productivity numbers is crucial but how do you do it? Gone are the days of tracking productivity numbers on pieces of paper. Technology now plays an essential role in the restaurant industry, and restaurant management software has made it easier than ever before for managers to make data-driven decisions. By using software to track inventory levels and turnover, monitor employee performance, and analyze customer data, managers can identify trends and opportunities for improvement. For example, with time and attendance tracking software, managers can easily track employee hours and identify areas where labor costs could be reduced. By adjusting schedules to better match demand, managers can eliminate unnecessary labor expenses. In addition, digital ordering systems can significantly reduce wait times and increase order accuracy, improving overall efficiency in the restaurant. Customers can now place their orders through a digital menu or kiosk, which is then sent directly to the kitchen. This can help reduce the amount of time servers spend taking orders and improve the accuracy of orders, reducing the need for re-dos and freebies. Furthermore, kitchen display systems can streamline kitchen operations and improve productivity by sending orders directly to a digital display in the kitchen. This eliminates the need for servers to physically deliver tickets and improves order accuracy. Managers can use this technology to track order completion times and staff productivity, allowing them to identify areas for improvement and optimize staffing levels.

Mobile apps are another essential tool that can provide staff with real-time access to their schedules, time clocks, and other important information. This improves communication and reduces the amount of time managers spend on administrative tasks. Employees can use a mobile app to clock in and out of shifts, view their schedule, and communicate with other staff members. By reducing the amount of time managers spend on administrative tasks, restaurants can improve overall efficiency and focus on more important matters.

If you're looking for inspiration on how to boost efficiency and profitability in the restaurant industry, look no further than the likes of Chipotle, Starbucks, and McDonald's. These industry giants have all faced challenges in the past, but by focusing on productivity metrics and using technology to their advantage, they have managed to overcome these hurdles and come out on top.

Take Chipotle, for example. Despite dealing with food safety concerns and negative press, the company managed to turn things around by prioritizing profitability. This meant cutting costs wherever possible, simplifying the menu, and streamlining the supply chain. By taking a proactive approach to improving labor efficiency, they were able to regain their status as a major player in the restaurant industry.

Starbucks also had its fair share of setbacks, with a decline in sales and profitability due to rapid expansion and an overly complex menu. But with a focus on productivity and efficiency, the coffee giant was able to bounce back. They implemented a productivity initiative that included streamlining the menu, optimizing the supply chain, and improving labor efficiency. By introducing technology such as mobile ordering and payment, Starbucks made it easier for customers to get their caffeine fix while reducing wait times.

And then there's McDonald's, the fast-food chain that needs no introduction. To maintain its dominance in the industry, the company invested in technology such as self-service kiosks and mobile ordering to reduce wait times and improve customer convenience. By analyzing productivity metrics like labor costs and inventory turnover, McDonald's was able to optimize its operations and improve profitability. And by streamlining the menu and improving supply chain efficiency, they were able to stay ahead of the competition.

These industry giants have shown us the path, but how do we embrace productivity metrics on a practical level? It's time to leverage technology. Integrate software that tracks metrics, optimizes labor costs, and streamlines operations. Imagine using digital ordering systems to slash wait times and enhance order accuracy. With mobile apps, empower your team with real-time access to schedules and essential information, freeing up more time for the work that truly matters.

So, here's the challenge: Embrace technology, dive deep into productivity metrics, and watch your restaurant evolve. Your journey to profit isn't just about revenue- it's about working smarter, creating an experience that dazzles customers, and fostering a thriving, innovative team. With the right tools and the right mindset, you will craft a recipe for success that's uniquely yours. Remember, the path to profit starts with mastering the art of productivity metrics.

Chapter 6: Manage your Costs or Else

As the old saying goes, "a small leak can sink a big ship." In the restaurant industry, this couldn't be more true. Even the most successful restaurants can be brought down by seemingly small financial leaks that go unnoticed or unaddressed. This underscores why managing a restaurant is an incredibly complex endeavor. It's not just about making a profit - it's about managing costs effectively to ensure your restaurant stays afloat. It demands for a blend of culinary mastery, hospitality finesse, marketing savvy, and financial acumen.

Frequently, restaurant owners and managers invest their energy, time, and resources into crafting menus, honing the atmosphere, and training their team, but fail to pay close attention to the financial details that can make or break their business. As you read through this chapter, our primary emphasis will be on the pivotal role of cost management. We'll uncover how even minor financial leaks can wield a significant influence on your overall profits. Additionally, we'll delve into the different types of costs that restaurants incur – from fixed costs like rent and utilities to variable ones like labor and food cost, and the effective methods to handle them. Don't worry, this chapter won't be a tedious exposition on accounting and finance. Instead, I'll be focusing on strategies to skillfully navigate these costs. I completely understand- dealing with numbers might not be the most thrilling aspect of the business, particularly for many of my fellow restaurateurs. My goal here is to help you grasp the concepts better. Why? Because whether we like to admit it or not, effectively managing costs in the restaurant industry involves more than just finances; it's intricately linked to operations. It's a skill set as essential as knowing how to set a table, cook a standout dish, or connect with customers. If you approach it with the same level of dedication and precision, it can truly become a key ingredient for your restaurant's success.

Imagine you're all set to embark on the journey of owning a brand-new restaurant. You've invested months envisioning the perfect menu, picturing a captivating ambiance, looking for the perfect location and conceiving what you believe will be a winning concept. Your vision is crystal clear, and now it's time to start making decisions and start turning those dreams into reality. As you dive into the decision-making process, the financial side of things takes center stage. Maybe some questions arise: What's a reasonable rent budget? What compensation should you offer your team? How should you price your menu items? What about the day-to-day operational expenses? And then comes the most daunting question: What level of profit must you achieve to keep your restaurant afloat? Suddenly, what was once an exciting adventure starts to morph into sleep-depriving worries. You realize you lack the expertise to confidently tackle these questions, and a sense of disorientation takes hold of your daily thoughts. Unfortunately, this sea of uncertainty often triggers a natural response – fear. And with fear comes a desire to rush through these decisions, hoping to swiftly move past the discomfort and onto the more desirable parts.

This, however, is where a significant stumbling block lies. It's one of the main reasons the success rate in this industry isn't as promising as we'd like. As we've already discussed in the first chapter, passion alone isn't enough. Rushing through these pivotal choices can cast a long shadow over your journey and may even perpetuate a cycle of less-than-optimal outcomes. So, think of this chapter as your trusted companion, guiding you past those nighttime fears, helping you emerge victorious, and genuinely embracing your dream. To achieve this, we need to start from the ground up- with the basics.

Basics of Costs

When it comes to costs, there are two primary categories: fixed costs and variable costs. Fixed costs are those expenses that stay constant, regardless of the volume of business you generate. These could encompass items such as rent, utilities, insurance, and property taxes. Although these costs are inherently "easier to manage," they are equally constrained by their inflexibility. It's this lack of adaptability of shifting with your business' ups and downs, that magnifies the impact of fixed costs on your financial bottom line. Think about this: When your rent is disproportionately high compared to your sales, it can start to nibble away at your profits, making the task of staying afloat more challenging.

In contrast, variable costs are the spending that fluctuates with the ebb and flow of your business' activity. Imagine essentials such as food, labor, and supplies. As your business becomes busier, it's only natural for your variable costs to ascend- assuming, of course, they were balanced to begin with. Given that these costs are intricately tied to your day-to-day operations, mastering their management is one of the most formidable challenges we, as restaurateurs, face. The difficulty stems from the ongoing struggle to keep them in check, given their susceptibility to external forces that are beyond our control, such as inflation in prices and hikes in minimum wages. Furthermore, internal factors come into play, aspects that we theoretically have control over, yet often necessitate substantial changes or reorganization of our daily operations and the individuals involved. Take, for instance, a scenario where your labor cost is unusually high. To address this, you might need to dig into your sales data to gauge if a resolution lies in adjusting your staffing levels or if you need to find ways to make your operations more efficient. On the flip side, you might already be operating with just the bare bones, in which case boosting sales could be the solution you're after.

To master the art of cost management, it's important to understand how to calculate them. This understanding will empower you to skillfully oversee your expenses and optimize your profitability. To lay a solid foundation, let's begin by delving into fixed costs, with a special focus on one pivotal element – rent. One of the most important factors to consider when opening a new restaurant is the amount of space you'll need, and how much you can afford to rent. Remember how we touched on the significance of selecting the right location earlier? We discussed how it's a blend of marketing and financial decision-making. Well, you are about to understand why that decision carries so much weight. As a young restaurateur, I learned this lesson the hard way. I was so excited about the idea of opening my own restaurant that I didn't think enough about the math behind my decision. I found a great location in the heart of Mexico City, signed the lease, and started renovating the space. But as the renovations progressed, reality hit me: I had based my sales analysis on the success of the restaurant in its local market without considering the challenges of being a new player in Mexico. Taking a step back and conducting a more thorough evaluation, I discovered a critical oversight: the space I had committed to for the next five years was much larger than necessary for my concept. I had underestimated the number of tables I needed to turn in order to generate enough sales that would turn a profit considering the necessity of covering my fixed costs, primarily the rent. I quickly realized that I had made a big mistake. With a large space to operate and a high rent to pay, I found it challenging to generate enough revenue to make a profit, and I was barely covering my costs. I learned a valuable lesson from this experience; as great as a location may be, it is vital to take the time to do some careful analysis of the space that will best suit your operation and how much you could afford to pay in rent. Discovering this magical number can be achieved through different methods, and it greatly depends on where you stand in your journey. But I'll be focusing on the most common two scenarios.

Scenario 1: You've Found Your Ideal Spot

More often than not, the journey of a restaurateur begins with the exciting discovery of an exceptional location. Whether it's through coincidental encounters while you're out and about, an unexpected proposal, or just sheer luck, you find yourself with a location that feels like the missing piece to bring your business dream to life. In such a situation, your primary task is to validate this by establishing your ideal table count.

The ideal table count signifies the number of tables and seats you should have in your restaurant to make everything work smoothly. This calculation takes into consideration a multitude of factors, encompassing available space, customer preferences, and your targeted revenue. Begin by evaluating the space at your disposal and envisioning the number of guests you'd like to comfortably accommodate simultaneously. When selecting table sizes – be it large or small – keep in mind the ambiance you wish to create. You will then have to estimate your table turnover time, which refers to how quickly a table becomes available again,– a practical technique involves dividing your opening hours into distinct meal periods. Subsequently, calculate how many tables you would need to turn per meal period to cover your rent costs. This process will allow you to determine whether this location is genuinely the right fit to fulfill your aspirations. Keep in mind the crucial necessity of finding a harmonious equilibrium between space and cost.

Scenario 2: You Have a Concept But No Venue
When figuring out how much rent to budget for a yet-to-be-chosen restaurant location, it's essential to forecast the potential earnings your establishment

could bring in. This is done by considering factors like the type of restaurant, the number of customers you expect, and the prices you plan to charge. To achieve this you'll have to determine two important values: your estimated average spend per guest and your ideal table count.

Estimating the average spending per guest involves forecasting how much money each guest is likely to spend during their time at your restaurant. To get started, you need to define your restaurant's concept and the type of cuisine you'll offer. Additionally, understanding your customer base- their preferences, demographics, and spending behaviors- is crucial. Once armed with this knowledge, the next step involves delving into market research. This means gathering insights from the local restaurant scene and studying competitors with similar concepts. This exploration will give you valuable information about what customers are willing to spend on comparable experiences in the current market.

Using these insights you can estimate what your average spend per guest will be. Ideally, you will go a step further and develop your menu and set prices during this phase. However, it's not always feasible due to time and resource constraints, especially when you're preparing for an opening. If you choose to skip this process, just keep the estimated average spending per guest in mind as you move forward.

Determining the ideal table count without a confirmed space calls for a slightly different approach. It involves a mix of educated guesses and research, and once you have a location in hand, you can fine-tune everything to match the actual layout. Start by considering your restaurant concept and the insights from your market research. Sketch out some layouts to help visualize different arrangements and scenarios. Also, think about your operating hours and how long customers might stay, which will help you estimate table turnover rates. This will ultimately help you work backward and calculate the amount of space you'll need. Armed with this knowledge, it is easier to make an informed decision about the size of the space you need and how much you can afford to pay in rent. A general guideline is to allocate around fourteen percent of your projected revenue for rent. You must remember, however, that rent is just a portion of your fixed expenses. Don't forget to consider other outlays like utilities, and operational costs such as marketing, legal fees, and equipment maintenance. While these aspects may differ among restaurants, their influence on your bottom line remains substantial.

Now, let's delve into variable costs and their calculation. As mentioned earlier in this chapter, these costs vary with your operations, making it essential to consistently monitor the outcomes of these calculations. Regrettably, this crucial practice often goes unnoticed, leading to ongoing losses that, may seem minor on their own but collectively can determine whether you're consistently wrestling with expenses or have the means to nurture your business' growth.

Managing Food Costs

One of the most important variable costs to track is your food costs. Food cost, put simply, refers to the cost of the ingredients used to prepare a dish. The calculation and monitoring of food cost hold great significance, as it will help you understand how much money is spent on ingredients and preparation for each dish. Armed with this information, you can make well-informed choices to ensure that menu prices not only offset costs but also yield profits. This practice also contributes to waste reduction, efficient menu management, early issue detection, and an evaluation of kitchen performance – all of which contribute to the overall success and profitability of your restaurant. Given this, crafting your menu stands out as one of the most crucial decision-making processes for your restaurant.

Menu design is a critical part of a restaurant's success, both in terms of customer satisfaction and financial performance. Crafting a menu is not just about listing savory dishes, it's about understanding the costs associated with each item. The ingredients, their quality, and the labor involved in preparation influence the pricing. Additionally, a pivotal aspect of menu design revolves around creating dishes that prove to be both popular and lucrative.

A well-thought-out menu strategy boosts profits by highlighting high-margin dishes, utilizing common ingredients across various items, and carefully controlling portion sizes to balance costs and customer satisfaction.

Even if a dish is beloved by customers, it might not be worth keeping on the menu if it doesn't generate enough profit. On the other hand, a less popular dish with a high profit margin could be a valuable addition. Striking the right balance between these factors allows you to create a menu that not only pleases your customers but also supports your bottom line.

In my experience, I've come to fully understand the pivotal role that menu design plays in determining the success of my establishments. As I took my first steps in the restaurant industry, I learned firsthand the profound impact that food costs can have on the bottom line. Despite having some customer-favorite dishes, upon closer examination of their food costs, I realized that their profitability was lacking. Acknowledging the need for a shift, I had to adjust accordingly. My first step was to eliminate some of the less profitable items, while giving prominence to dishes with higher profit margins. This simple but effective move helped elevate my overall profitability. But I wasn't content with just that; I wanted to create new menu items that were both delectable and cost-effective. This is where my experimentation with new dishes, like arancini, came into play. Arancini, a traditional Italian delicacy made of risotto balls filled with cheese, seemed like a risky endeavor due to its labor-intensive nature. However, I recognized that although the raw materials for arancini were expensive, it was a better option than importing proteins from the United States to make the chicken wings or fried calamari we originally had on the menu. Additionally, we could leverage the fact that labor costs in Mexico were more competitive. This revelation gave me the confidence to take the leap. The result was a resounding success. Arancini turned out to be a mouthwatering and affordable appetizer that my customers absolutely adored. Not only did it delight their taste buds, but it also proved to be a highly profitable addition to my menu. Since they could be made in bulk, planned production was straightforward, and the low raw material costs allowed me to sell them at a significantly higher markup compared to the other less profitable appetizers. Arancini not only bolstered my profitability but also gave it a unique and creative edge. Customers were excited to try the latest appetizers, and as word-of-mouth recommendations spread like wildfire, we began attracting more customers. By diligently analyzing my food costs and fearlessly experimenting with new dishes, I achieved an impressive surge in profitability and crafted a restaurant that stood out from the competition.

My advice: don't shy away from thinking outside the box. Sometimes, the most delectable and profitable dishes require a little extra effort to create, but the rewards are well worth it.

Having said that, it remains essential not to lose sight of your customers' preferences. I had an appetizer on my menu that was immensely popular, but the food cost was a staggering sixty percent. I initially priced it this way as a hook to attract new customers but after a few months, I recognized the need to change it. I made a few strategic tweaks, switched some ingredients, and managed to reduce the food cost to a more competitive thirty percent. This transformation was not only gratifying but also served as a testament to my ability to harmonize my customers' tastes with my financial objectives. Mastering the art of menu design requires a judicious blend of creativity, data analysis, and understanding customer preferences. It's a journey of discovery, where experimenting with new dishes and optimizing food costs can lead to phenomenal outcomes.

Beyond assisting you in making informed decisions about your product mix, adopting a cost-based approach to your menu design process will also reveal another vital figure for your financial well-being: your theoretical cost. Theoretical food cost is the calculated ideal cost that a restaurant should incur to prepare and serve a particular dish, assuming zero wastage, spoilage, or theft, and precise utilization of ingredients. Therefore this concept is closely tied to effective control of real food costs and inventory. Real food costs can differ from theoretical costs due to reasons like ingredient wastage during preparation and storage, variations in portion sizes, differences in ingredient quality, staff theft, recipe modifications, operational inefficiencies, and more. These real-world operational factors can lead to higher actual food costs, directly affecting the expected profit from your menu. This is precisely why monitoring your food cost is such a critical practice. Effectively managing it entails identifying and addressing these discrepancies to control expenses and operate a more efficient business.

Inventory Management

All this theory sounds promising, doesn't it? But the real challenge is how to put it into practice. How can we spot and fix these small leaks while juggling numerous responsibilities? Well, apart from making data analysis a priority, there are other strategies and tools at your disposal to effectively manage your food cost. One tool that will encompass a significant portion of your operational process is inventory management. Inventory management involves keeping track of and controlling the food and drink items that your restaurant needs. This means predicting how much of each item will be used, ordering it, checking its quality when it arrives, storing it properly, and using it efficiently to avoid wasting food and money. Think of it as ensuring your kitchen always has the right ingredients on hand at the right times, all while keeping costs in check and providing consistent dishes to your customers. Within this fine-tuned equilibrium restaurateurs face a formidable challenge: buying the right quantity of food. You don't want to end up with too much stock, yet you definitely don't want to hear the dreaded term "eighty-six". In the restaurant realm, "eighty-six" is code for "we're out of that item." And when your kitchen staff utters those words, it can translate to lost revenue, unhappy diners, and a hit to your reputation. Let me give you a glimpse into how inventory management played out in my own business, so you can better understand how I found my balance.

As a new restaurant owner, I was blissfully unaware of the impact that neglecting inventory management could have on my business. I figured that as long as the food was delicious and customers were happy, the business would take care of itself. Oh boy, was I wrong. It wasn't until a few months into running my restaurant that I realized how much I had neglected inventory management. We were constantly overstocked with ingredients that we didn't need, and items were expiring or going to waste. To make matters worse, we were losing money from employee theft. I started to panic, realizing that I needed to take action to turn things around. So, I brought my team together, and collectively, we crafted a solid plan to efficiently handle inventory and supplies. Our initial move involved closely monitoring the inventory levels of every ingredient and setting per stock levels according to our weekly usage. Additionally, we implemented a system for ordering supplies on a regular schedule, ensuring a well-maintained stock without excessive inventory.

This strategy allowed us to avoid overstocking while ensuring that we always had enough supplies to meet customer demand.

Another essential aspect of our inventory management strategy was the constant overseeing of the "First In, First Out" (FIFO) rotation method for perishables. We made sure that our staff used the oldest products first to prevent spoilage. This simple yet effective approach not only helped us maintain the quality of our food but also significantly reduced food waste, leading to substantial long-term savings. I won't deny that this process required significant time and effort, but the results were truly worth it. Moreover, by taking a strong stance against theft, we set a precedent of zero tolerance for dishonest practices within our organization. By staying committed to disciplined inventory management, we not only controlled our expenses but also upheld the quality of our dishes and built a sustainable foundation. The most rewarding part? It led us to profitability and to run a thriving restaurant. Of course, mastering this tool required discipline, meticulous attention to detail, and the courage to make tough decisions. Yet armed with effective strategies and an unwavering commitment to efficient inventory practices, you can absolutely take control of costs and boost your bottom line.

Variable Costs

So far, we've discussed the internal elements of food cost that are within your control, to actively improve the management of your restaurant's variable costs. However, as previously mentioned, one of the main reasons that makes this challenging is the vulnerability of variable costs to external influences. In the context of food cost, this refers to price increases and shortages. While these two factors might appear beyond your control, there are still strategies you can employ to better navigate them.

One important strategy I learned from an early age in business is that of building relationships. These lessons have proven to be my greatest assets in the restaurant industry. Building strong relationships with vendors can significantly impact food costs. By fostering positive connections, you can actually negotiate better prices for ingredients and supplies, leading to increased profits. These trusted relationships can also guarantee a consistent supply of high-quality products, reducing the risk of waste and customer dissatisfaction. In addition to that, it can help lock in stable prices over the long term, making your operations smoother, cutting down on administrative hassles, and giving you more control over your food costs.

Negotiating with suppliers, however, is only winning a small battle. One of the biggest enemies of this industry are the last-minute purchases. These seemingly innocent last-minute decisions can significantly affect food costs and the smooth functioning of our operations. When restaurants buy ingredients last minute, they often pay higher prices and end up with more food waste due to overbuying or choosing lower-quality items. These rushed purchases can disrupt menu consistency, compromise food quality, and strain kitchen staff. I grasped this concept swiftly. As I started tackling this challenge, it became apparent that it revolved more around cultivating a particular mindset than simply fulfilling operational requirements. The culture within your restaurant team plays a crucial role in cost management. As a result, my focus shifted to fostering a culture of awareness and resourcefulness among my team. It became essential to educate them about the importance of managing inventory effectively and controlling costs. I took the initiative to provide training on our internal systems, which were designed to meticulously monitor every incoming and outgoing item in the kitchen. The core of this mindset rested on the essential need for proactive planning, discouraging any last-minute purchases. Collaborating with my leadership team, we established clear expectations and targets regarding inventory management and cost reduction. Each team member was entrusted with accountability for their role in driving us toward these goals.

Through this shared dedication to cost control and mindful decision-making, we successfully avoided emergency purchases and kept our food costs in check. Granted, it wasn't always effortless, and tough decisions regarding menu items or ingredients had to be made at times. However, we always kept our focus on the bigger picture—sustainable revenue growth. Our dedication to controlling food costs and evading last-minute purchases allowed us to witness tangible results. The increased profits we achieved were reinvested back into the restaurant, contributing to its long-term success and growth.

To my fellow restaurateurs who rely solely on revenue and believe that high revenue can solve everything, I want to emphasize that success extends beyond high revenue; it hinges on sustainable revenue.

An approach to success rooted in awareness and cost-consciousness not only enhances your bottom line but also solidifies your restaurant's reputation as a consistent provider of exceptional dining experiences. Cost management isn't a solitary task; rather, it stands as a foundational element within a comprehensive strategy that lays the path for long-lasting success.

Revisiting the primary subject of variable costs and their calculations, the next pivotal aspect in cost management is labor cost. As a restaurant owner, you need to be well aware of how efficiently managing your labor cost can significantly impact your bottom line. I remember facing this struggle early on in my career, trying to strike the right balance between staffing enough employees to meet demand while also keeping costs in check. It wasn't until I took a step back and evaluated my labor expenses that I could implement strategies to manage costs more effectively.

To begin this evaluation, having a clear understanding of the diverse components that make up labor costs is essential. It extends beyond mere base pay and the familiar additional costs such as overtime pay, benefits, and payroll taxes. Often, there are other costs that tend to be overlooked, like premium pay (relevant during holidays or specific shifts), training expenditures, costs associated with turnover, uniform expenses, provisions for staff meals, compensation for paid breaks and downtime, administrative hours, initiatives for employee incentives, investments in technology and tools, and unproductive hours that also need to be taken into account. By breaking down these expenses, you gain a better understanding of your labor costs, enabling you to take necessary steps to control them.

Aside from understanding the components of your labor cost, another pivotal element in the successful management of labor costs involves crafting efficient employee schedules. Initially, I fell into the trap of overstaffing, thinking that it would translate to better service. However, I soon learned that having too many employees simultaneously led to inefficiency and reduced productivity, negatively impacting employee morale. In my effort to address these issues, I initially resorted to reducing labor, only to then swing to the opposite extreme and find myself understaffed. This experience taught me that operating with inadequate staff can just as much lead to a downward spiral of negative consequences that can affect your restaurant's reputation, employee satisfaction, customer experience, and financial health. To find the right balance, I started tracking customer traffic patterns and business trends. By doing so, I was able to schedule employees more efficiently, thereby reducing labor costs without compromising service quality.

Achieving this balance is crucial for ensuring the profitability of your restaurant.

But managing labor costs isn't just about technical know-how; creating a positive work environment is equally important. As discussed in chapter four, having a positive company culture can significantly improve job satisfaction and reduce turnover. Employee turnover can have a big impact on your labor cost and your customer experience. When employees leave, the restaurant incurs expenses related to recruitment and training of new staff. New employees are often not as fast or as good at their jobs as experienced ones, potentially reducing the restaurant's efficiency and increasing the likelihood of errors. Moreover, customer dissatisfaction may arise if they get the wrong orders or bad service. High turnover could also lead to increased overtime expenses, as well as heightened investments of time and resources in the hiring and training processes. Ultimately, high turnover can pose challenges for the restaurant's profitability and its ability to provide customers with a satisfying experience.

While there is undeniable difficulty in managing labor costs, a challenge that has become even more pronounced in a post-pandemic area, we have a valuable ally in this struggle: technology. Leveraging technological tools to optimize labor management is paramount. This spans from software capable of generating schedules aligned with peak restaurant hours, monitoring employee shifts, and forecasting busy periods, to point-of-sale systems that assist in budgeting, reporting, and training. There are plenty of resources available to help you keep track of labor costs and keep employees motivated. The goal is to manage labor costs effectively without compromising on quality or customer service. With well-balanced strategies in place, you can save money while keeping your employees happy and engaged.

Financial Management

Finally, no discussion of cost management would be complete without emphasizing the significance of financial management in controlling expenses. Within the restaurant industry, financial management skills are a key driver of success, encompassing budgeting, cash flow management, financial reporting, and debt management. These skills are essential for achieving long-term success and sustainable profitability. Effective budgeting, in particular, serves as a cornerstone of cost management. Without a budget in place, you run the risk of exceeding your earnings with your expenditures. A well-structured budget became my guiding tool, enabling me to not only monitor expenses but also anticipate future cash flows. This proactive approach empowered me to make informed decisions regarding investments and expenses. It's important to prioritize essential expenses such as rent, utilities, and payroll, ensuring that they receive top priority in your budget. Afterward, allocate funds for other crucial costs like marketing or supplies. It's vital to establish a hierarchy in your budget to ensure that these critical areas are adequately funded. Moreover, remember that budgets should not be set in stone. Regularly review your budget and be ready to make adjustments as needed. This flexibility will allow you to adapt to unexpected changes and maintain financial stability within the dynamic landscape of the restaurant industry.

Similarly, cash flow management holds immense importance in the restaurant industry. I vividly remember a challenging moment when I had to unexpectedly close my restaurant for a few weeks due to unforeseen circumstances. During this time, the wisdom of prudent cash flow management became abundantly clear. By having sufficient reserves in place, I was able to navigate the temporary closure without accumulating additional debt, ensuring the long-term financial health of my establishment. Cash flow management, in essence, involves monitoring the inflow and outflow of money in your restaurant. This entails not only tracking revenue and expenses but also considering factors like seasonality, supplier payment terms, and customer payment habits. A positive cash flow, where your inflows exceed your outflows, is essential for the day-to-day operations and growth of your restaurant. Moreover, cash flow management is crucial for seizing opportunities and addressing unforeseen challenges. It allows you to invest in restaurant improvements, expand, and withstand unexpected setbacks without compromising your financial stability. Therefore, just as with budgeting, regularly reviewing and adjusting your cash flow management strategies is vital to ensure your restaurant's financial well-being.

Alongside budgeting and cash flow management, financial reporting is of special importance for restaurant owners. Regularly reviewing financial reports enables you to identify areas where costs can be reduced and profits can be increased. Performing financial analysis and monitoring key performance indicators (KPIs) is crucial for making well-founded decisions about your restaurant's financial performance. For instance, I constantly monitored food and beverage cost percentages, labor cost percentages, and net profit margins to uncover opportunities for enhancing profitability. This data-driven analysis informed decisions on pricing strategies, menu design, and staffing levels. Ongoing financial analysis and data management are paramount components in achieving lasting success in the restaurant industry. These essential practices will be further detailed in the following chapter.

As we conclude this chapter, one central truth emerges: cost control serves as the linchpin to unlocking success and maximizing profitability in the dynamic world of the restaurant industry. Beyond crafting an exceptional menu and delivering top-notch service, prudent expense management and unwavering focus on your bottom line are equally indispensable. Yet, the most pivotal takeaway from this chapter is that managing costs transcends mere cost-cutting; it revolves around the art of operating with greater efficiency, profitability, and effectiveness—all while upholding the standards of quality and customer service.

Chapter 7:

Leverage your Data

The restaurant industry is undeniably competitive, and in this cutthroat environment, would it surprise you to know that the secret to your success lies within your own data? Embracing the power of business intelligence is crucial for restaurant owners to make intelligent and data-driven decisions that can lead to triumph in this challenging landscape. With slim margins, unpredictable customer preferences, and rising operational costs, juggling multiple moving parts can be overwhelming, making it challenging to stay on top of everything and make informed choices. However, the strategic use of business intelligence can simplify this complexity and provide you with a competitive advantage.

Business Intelligence

At its core, business intelligence is the practice of collecting, analyzing, and utilizing data to drive decision-making. By harnessing data insights, restaurant owners can gain a deeper understanding of their operations, uncover valuable trends, and optimize various aspects of their business, ultimately leading to streamlined operations and increased profitability. In this chapter, I provide practical guidance on how restaurant owners can effectively use business intelligence to gain a competitive edge in the market. We will delve into essential topics such as data analysis, custom solution development, project management, and the future of information management in the restaurant industry. As we explore these concepts, I will continue to share real-life examples from my experiences as an entrepreneur. I wholeheartedly believe that storytelling is a powerful tool for learning and inspiration, and I hope that you will find these stories engaging and relatable, providing valuable insights and practical takeaways. By the end of this chapter, you will have a comprehensive understanding of business intelligence and its transformative potential for your restaurant business and your life. Armed with this knowledge, you will be well-equipped to make data-driven decisions, identify opportunities for improvement, and implement custom solutions that align with your unique business objectives. Embracing the power of business intelligence will not only help you navigate the complexities of the restaurant industry but also position your establishment for sustainable growth and long-term success and allow you to manage your business effectively without the need to sacrifice your precious time. So let's embark on this journey together and unlock the full potential of your restaurant's data-driven future.

As a restaurant owner, you know that success in the industry requires hard work, dedication, and a lot of trial and error. But what if there was a way to make your job easier, to make decisions with confidence, and to stay ahead of the competition? This is where business intelligence comes in. Business intelligence is about using data to inform decision-making. By collecting and analyzing information about your business, you can gain insights into customer preferences, operational inefficiencies, and opportunities for growth. But leveraging business intelligence is more than just collecting data. It's about actually using that data to drive action.

By identifying trends and patterns in your data, you can create custom solutions that address the specific needs of your business.

This could mean changing your menu offerings, adjusting your pricing strategy, or streamlining your supply chain. One of the most compelling reasons to embrace business intelligence is the ability to identify opportunities for improvement. Every restaurant has areas that could benefit from optimization, whether it's reducing wait times, improving food quality, or enhancing the overall dining experience. By analyzing data from various sources, such as sales records, customer feedback, and employee performance metrics, restaurant owners can identify these areas and develop targeted solutions.

Business intelligence can help you identify these opportunities. Let's say, for example, that you notice a trend in your sales data- your lunch rush is always busy, but your dinner service is slow. By digging deeper into the data, you might find that customers are waiting too long for their food during dinner service, leading to negative reviews and lost business. Armed with this information, you can make changes to your kitchen operations to speed up dinner service and improve customer satisfaction. The benefits of information management go beyond just operational improvements. By using a data-driven approach to decision-making, restaurant owners can make better choices and mitigate risk. For example, let's say you're considering adding a new menu item. By leveraging your data, you can analyze sales data to determine which items are most popular and which are likely to be successful. This reduces the risk of introducing a new menu item that doesn't resonate with customers and ultimately leads to wasted resources and lost profits. Business intelligence can also help you stay ahead of the competition. By using data to identify trends in the market, you can adapt your business strategy to meet changing customer needs and preferences. For example, if you notice a trend towards plant-based diets, you can adjust your menu offerings to include more vegetarian and vegan options.

Businesses in other industries have already discovered the power of information management. Retailers use data to optimize their supply chain and improve inventory management. Healthcare providers use data to track patient outcomes and identify areas for improvement. In the restaurant industry, business intelligence is becoming increasingly important as competition continues to grow. Leveraging business intelligence is a powerful endeavor for all businesses looking to achieve success and maximize profitability. Let's explore the first step in information management - data analysis.

Types of Data Collection

Data analysis is the most important step in information management, but before you can start using data to make informed decisions, you need to collect and analyze the right data. Let's first explore the various types of data that you can collect and analyze, and how to use this data to gain insights into the business. There are many different types of data that restaurant owners can collect and analyze, but all data falls into one of three categories:

customer, business, and employee data. Understanding your customer data means understanding your customers and is critical to the success of your restaurant. By collecting data on customer preferences, you can identify popular menu items, track customer feedback, and develop promotions and loyalty programs that keep customers coming back. Some examples of data you can collect include customer demographics, menu item popularity, and customer feedback surveys.

Business data is another vital piece of information for restaurant owners. Business data is all the data pertinent to your restaurant. This data includes sales trends, average check, online sales, third party sales, discounts, cancellations, waste logs, production logs and inventories. By tracking business data like sales trends, for example, you can identify which menu items are selling well and which are not, and adjust your menu and pricing accordingly. You can also use sales data to track revenue and profit margins, and identify areas for cost savings. Each unique

176

piece of data will allow you to identify inefficiencies, discrepancies and opportunities to reduce your costs or grow your business.

The third type of data you can collect is employee data. Your employees are a key part of your restaurant's success, so it's important to track their performance. Some examples of data you can collect include employee attendance records, sales performance, and customer satisfaction ratings. By analyzing this data, you can identify areas for employee training and development, and recognize top performers.

Collecting Data

There are many different methods for collecting all this data, but the most common is your restaurant's point of sale system (POS). Even the most basic POS system has most of the basic reporting capabilities discussed. Your point of sale system is a valuable tool for collecting sales data. Most modern

POS systems can track sales by menu item, time of day, and even employee, providing valuable insights into your business. Many POS systems also offer employee performance tracking, allowing you to collect data on sales performance and customer satisfaction ratings. On occasions, depending on the information you want to analyze, you may have to create custom structures in excel to gather your desired data. Collecting data is necessary to make informed decisions about your restaurant business, however, collecting data is only half the battle. Data without the proper analysis is just a collection of useless numbers and figures.

Data analysis can be a daunting task, especially for those who are not familiar with statistical analysis methods. Fortunately, there are many different tools and techniques available to help you make sense of your data. It doesn't matter what specific tool you utilize, the important thing is that you use one. Just in case you don't have a favorite method, I will discuss the most common methods for analyzing data.

Analyzing Data

Data Visualization is one of the most popular and effective ways to analyze data. Data visualization tools, such as charts and graphs, can help you make sense of complex data sets and identify trends and patterns. For example, if you're trying to track your restaurant's sales over time, you can use a line chart to plot your sales data over a period of months or years. This will allow you to see if there are any seasonal trends or if sales have been increasing or decreasing over time. There are many different types of data visualization tools, each with their own unique strengths and weaknesses. Here are a few examples: bar charts, pie charts, and line charts. Bar charts are a simple yet effective way to visualize data. They can be used to compare different categories of data, such as the sales of different menu items or the number of customers served on different days of the week. Pie charts are another common type of chart that can be used to visualize data. They are particularly useful for showing how different categories of data relate to each other. For example, you could use a pie chart to show what percentage of your restaurant's revenue comes from different menu items. Line charts are ideal for tracking trends over time. They can be used to plot data points over a period of days, weeks, or months. For example, you could use a line chart to track your restaurant's sales over the course of a year.

Another common method for analyzing data is doing a statistical analysis. This involves using statistical techniques to quantify the relationships between different variables and identify statistically significant trends. For example, you could use statistical analysis to determine whether there is a relationship between the number of employees working at your restaurant and the amount of revenue generated. Regression analysis is another powerful tool for predicting future trends based on historical data. It allows you to identify the relationship between two or more variables and use that information to make predictions about future outcomes. For example, you could use regression analysis to predict how changes in your restaurant's menu prices might affect sales. Data analysis is about identifying patterns in your business. Regardless of the tool or methodology used, the idea is to gain valuable insights into your business operations and make informed decisions that will help you maximize profitability.

I didn't always analyze the data for my restaurant, but once I began, it is now hard to imagine managing a restaurant any other way. Without analysis of your particular data, you are just making decisions based on trial and error. Picture this scenario, you notice that a particular dish on the menu isn't selling well, and you know you need to find out why. You decide to collect data on customer preferences, using surveys and social media analysis to determine what customers are looking for. To stay competitive in this industry, it's important to keep an eye on customer preferences and adapt to changing trends. The data shows that customers are increasingly interested in healthier options, so you rework the recipe to create a healthier version of the dish. You also adjust the menu description to highlight the healthier ingredients and preparation methods. As a result, the dish quickly becomes a customer favorite and your sales are boosted.

Personally, my favorite use of data analysis was for cost control. Managing labor costs, for example, used to be a major challenge for me. I decided to collect data on employee performance, including timekeeping and productivity. The data revealed that certain employees were consistently taking longer breaks than others, clocking in late or not being productive during their whole eight hour shift. All these factors contributed to the high labor costs. I addressed this issue by implementing a more structured break schedule, a system for disincentivizing tardiness and a new labor structure with reduced hour shifts. I also provided training to employees on the importance of time management. As a result, I was able to drastically reduce labor costs without sacrificing service quality.

As restaurant owners, we're constantly looking for ways to improve our business and maximize profitability. Fortunately, with the right data analysis and custom solutions, you can identify areas for improvement and implement changes that will benefit your business in the long run. Data analysis can help you identify areas where your business could improve. For example, if you notice that your restaurant is consistently slow during certain hours of the day, you can analyze customer traffic patterns to determine the cause. Maybe there's a competing restaurant nearby that's drawing customers away during those hours, or perhaps there's a lack of foot traffic in the area during that time of day.

By identifying the problem, you can develop custom solutions to address it.

Developing Data-Driven Solutions

Once you've identified areas for improvement, it's time to develop custom solutions to address them. This process can involve anything from adjusting your menu to revamping your marketing strategy to improving your restaurant's overall operations. It's important to involve your employees in this process, as they may have valuable insights and suggestions for improving the business. Make sure your employees understand why the changes are being made and how they will benefit the business. By communicating changes effectively, you'll help build trust with your employees and ensure a smooth transition to the new way of doing things.

By involving them in the process, you'll also help them feel invested in the success of the restaurant. Remember what you learned in chapters three and four. Your team is a key factor for your restaurant business to thrive.

Implementation

Now that you've identified the key areas for improvement and developed custom solutions to address them, it's time to implement those solutions with your team and manage your data on an ongoing basis. Some solutions may only require training, others may be more complex and may also require the use of tools and software solutions or the coordination of different members of your team. Implementing custom solutions with your employees requires effective project management techniques. Here are a few key steps to follow:

1. Set Goals: Clearly define the goals and objectives of the project. Make sure everyone involved understands what you're trying to achieve.

2. Create a Plan: Develop a plan for implementing the solution. This should include timelines, budget, resource allocation, and specific tasks and responsibilities.

3. Communicate: Communicate the plan to all stakeholders, including employees, vendors, and customers. Make sure everyone knows what is expected of them.

4. Monitor Progress: Monitor progress regularly to ensure the project stays on track. Make adjustments as needed.

Change can be difficult, especially in a busy restaurant environment. In my experience, I have used these three things to help manage the transition: involve employees, train employees and celebrate milestones. You must involve employees in the process and communicate the changes to them early on. Make sure you ask for their input and feedback, employees must feel invested in the new project. Make sure employees understand the new processes and procedures by providing training and support as needed. Last but certainly not least, celebrate all successes and milestones along the way by recognizing all employees who have contributed to the success of the project. These three strategies will effectively help manage any transition smoothly.

It is important to ensure that your custom solutions are sustainable over the long-term. Perhaps the most important aspect of this is to regularly monitor the performance of your solutions to ensure they're meeting your goals. If the solution is not working, it's ok to go back and make adjustments as needed to ensure the solution remains effective. Even if the solution is effective, make it a habit to collect feedback from your employees to identify areas for improvement. Your employees are a key component in effective project management and change management within your organization.

Achieving success in this industry demands an astute approach to business intelligence. Throughout my journey, I've witnessed firsthand the remarkable impact of effective data analysis and management in shaping a thriving business. Allow me to jump into a few personal case studies that exemplify the transformative potential of business intelligence for my business.

Case Study 1: Elevating Service Quality

In the early days of my flagship restaurant situated in a bustling tourist destination in Mexico City, we faced challenges with inconsistent service quality and dwindling customer satisfaction. Realizing that operational improvements were imperative to stay competitive, I embarked on a journey of data collection and analysis. We carefully examined customer feedback and employee performance metrics, discovering that high turnover, inconsistent training, and communication gaps between front and back of house staff were hindering our service. To address these issues, we introduced a comprehensive training program, prioritizing communication, teamwork, and exceptional customer service. In parallel, we adopted a cutting-edge data management system that facilitated real-time feedback from both customers and employees. This dynamic approach allowed us to identify areas for improvement on a weekly basis, enabling prompt and effective action.

The results were tangible and immediately rewarding. Within a year, customer reviews improved by thirty percent, and our restaurant became a top-rated destination in one of the busiest areas of Mexico City. The key takeaway here is that prioritizing effective data management and communication led us to a deeper understanding of operational challenges, which ultimately enhanced customer satisfaction and increased our profitability. Simple solutions, rooted in data insights, can yield substantial and enduring results.

Case Study 2: Streamlining Supply Chain

As my restaurant empire expanded, controlling costs and optimizing supply chain management became even more vital. I discovered that my restaurants were grappling with high food waste and inventory expenses. To tackle this, we meticulously analyzed sales and inventory data, discerning popular and underperforming menu items, as well as areas of waste and excess. Drawing from this analysis, we devised a new menu that focused on the most popular items while eliminating underperforming ones to reduce waste. Additionally, we introduced a real-time inventory management system, empowering us to track inventory levels and waste with precision. These strategic changes resulted in a remarkable 37% reduction in food waste and an astonishing 19% increase in profitability.

Moreover, we saw this newly developed menu as a powerful marketing tool. By leveraging our menu revamp, we reached out to media allies and worked on a remarkable remarketing public relations campaign. The key takeaway here is that effective supply chain management, supported by data-driven decision-making, was essential for reducing waste and improving efficiency.

Case Study 3: Strengthening Marketing Strategies

As we sought to solidify our brand in Mexico, we faced stiff competition and dwindling sales. Realizing the importance of an enhanced marketing strategy, we began on a data collection mission, seeking valuable insights into customer demographics, preferences, and behaviors. Armed with these data-driven insights, we crafted a new marketing strategy concentrating on bolstering our online presence through social media and online reviews. Additionally, we implemented a loyalty program that rewarded frequent visits to retain existing customers. The outcome was obvious: our online presence flourished, attracting a wave of new customers, while the loyalty program ensured we retained our valued patrons, propelling us to new heights of profitability.

The main takeaway from this case study is that a robust marketing strategy, grounded in data analysis, was essential for attracting and retaining customers, especially in a highly competitive market. By leveraging your own data, businesses can craft tailored marketing plans that resonate with their target audience. These real-life case studies exemplify the tremendous impact of effective data management on achieving business success. By analyzing data, identifying opportunities, crafting custom solutions, and perpetually managing data, we have the tools to revolutionize our businesses and achieve sustainable profitability.

Remember that the solutions to common business challenges need not be complex or costly. Often, simple tweaks to our operations, guided by data insights, can result in significant gains for our restaurants.

I hope these personal stories inspire and motivate you to embrace the power of business intelligence in your own journey.

The cold reality is that the restaurant industry is a competitive environment that requires smart, data-driven decision-making in order to succeed. Business intelligence can simplify the complex process of managing your business and frees your time so that you can live a balanced life. By leveraging data insights, you can gain a competitive edge, streamline your operations, and increase profitability. Put simply, business intelligence has the potential to transform both your businesses and your life and ultimately, isn't that what we want? I wholeheartedly believe that this is one of the most underutilized and undervalued tools in our business.

Chapter 8:

The Ultimate Cheat Code

As we conclude our journey, I'd like to close with a chapter dedicated to sharing the most valuable lessons I've learned. These insights go beyond conventional and technical business advice. Regardless of where you stand in your entrepreneurial journey or the specific type of business you have, in the following pages, we will discover the real cheat code to lasting success.

Over the years, as an entrepreneur, I have come to understand that running a profitable and sustainable business is not just about strategy, planning, and the day-to-day aspects of the operation. It's about cultivating a mindset within yourself and your team that is resilient, adaptable, and deeply creative.

The ultimate secret to success lies within you; it is the mastery of your own mindset.

As entrepreneurs, we inevitably face setbacks, failures, and unforeseen changes that can be disheartening. Yet it's not the challenges themselves that will ultimately dictate our fate; it's our response to them. How we navigate these trials will ultimately determine our success. That's precisely why it is essential to develop a mindset capable of turning challenges into opportunities and setbacks into a launching pad for growth. As Henry Ford so aptly put it, "whether you think you can or think you can't, you're right." This statement holds a profound truth for entrepreneurs like us. We all face trials on our path to success, but the ability to overcome them is what can set us apart as those who achieve their goals rather than those who don't. And at the core of this ability lies our mindset.

While it's certainly important to possess business knowledge and skills, I am convinced that our attitude, mindset, and outlook on life are equally, if not more, important for achieving success.

Fixed Mindset vs. Growth Mindset

Our Mindset is the lens through which we see the world. It's made up of our beliefs, attitudes, and assumptions, and it influences how we think and act. Let's begin by understanding the two primary mindsets that shape our approach to challenges: the fixed mindset and the growth mindset. Those with a fixed mindset tend to believe that their abilities and traits are set in stone, unable to be changed. Consequently, they interpret failure as proof of their limitations and shy away from taking risks. On the other hand, individuals with a growth mindset view their abilities as malleable, capable of being developed through hard work, determination, and a willingness to learn from their mistakes. They see obstacles not as roadblocks but as opportunities to expand their skills and knowledge, making them more inclined to embrace challenges and take calculated risks. It is this growth mindset that grants them resilience in the face of setbacks, enabling them to perceive failure as an opportunity for improvement rather than a judgment of their capabilities. In the world of business, having a growth mindset can make all the difference.

Consider the inspiring story of Steve Jobs, who, after being fired from the company he co-founded, could have succumbed to defeat. Instead, he embraced the growth mindset, seeing his setback as an opportunity to embark on a new venture, NeXT, which eventually led to his triumphant return to Apple and the creation of revolutionary products. Similarly, Colonel Sanders faced countless rejections in the market before finding success with his concept, Kentucky Fried Chicken. Rather than accepting failure as a final verdict, he harnessed a growth mindset, refining his recipe until he achieved greatness.

The key to cultivating a growth mindset lies in shifting our focus from the outcome to the process. Embrace challenges, welcome feedback, and continuously seek opportunities to learn and improve.

On your entrepreneurial journey, understanding and cultivating this growth mindset is the foundation of your success. To do so, you must confront one of the most significant obstacles many entrepreneurs face- the fear of failure.

Do I Fear Failure?

The fear of failure can be immobilizing, preventing us from taking risks and exploring new possibilities. However, it's vital to understand that failure is not only part of the process but also an essential aspect of growth and achievement.

By reframing failure as a valuable teacher, we can transform fear into curiosity and experimentation.

Successful entrepreneurs have learned the art of *failing forward*, acknowledging that failures are not dead ends but stepping stones on the path to triumph. The concept of *failing forward* involves the continuous process of learning and growing from our mistakes, cultivating resilience, and resolutely pursuing our goals. Instead of giving up when things go wrong, this mindset invites us to transform these obstacles into valuable lessons, adapt our strategies, and forge ahead with a positive mindset. It's the belief that failure is not the end but rather a springboard to success.

Another strategy that can help you cultivate a growth mindset is the concept of *failing fast*. This approach encourages individuals to embrace challenges, extract valuable lessons from mistakes, and view setbacks as opportunities for improvement rather than ignoring or avoiding them. It places importance on actively seeking feedback, displaying resilience in the face of failure, and persistently working towards solutions. By practicing *failing fast*, you not only increase your adaptability and willingness to learn but also reinforce the belief that your abilities can be developed through effort and experience.

By embracing the mindset that failure is an invaluable opportunity to learn, grow, and refine your strategies, you can develop a growth mindset that empowers you.

This book itself is a testament to the power of failing forward, as every setback I encountered in my journey became an opportunity for growth, exploration, and innovation. I built a successful food and beverage consulting business by learning from the setbacks I encountered in my own restaurant business. Through the process of recognizing areas that need improvement and implementing more effective systems, I put that expertise to good use by helping fellow restaurateurs maximize their own success.

Conquering Your Limiting Beliefs

Sometimes, even with a growth mindset, we may still find ourselves grappling with our own limiting beliefs- those deeply ingrained notions that restrict our potential and hinder us from reaching our goals. These beliefs take various forms, from feeling inadequate to thinking success is unattainable, or believing we lack the ability to learn new skills. Likely originating from early experiences and external influences, these limiting beliefs, when internalized, can persist in our subconscious, subtly sabotaging our progress. But, the good news is, we have the power to overcome these self-imposed limitations.

The first step is to shine a light on our limiting beliefs, no matter how deeply buried they may be.

To uncover our limiting beliefs, it's essential to pay close attention and become self-aware of our thoughts and emotions. This process allows us to gradually unearth the beliefs that hinder us, preventing us from reaching our full potential. Once these beliefs are identified, we must take the courageous step of challenging and confronting them directly.

One potent strategy to challenge them is to search for evidence that contradicts these beliefs. For instance, if we doubt our capacity to thrive in business, we can seek instances throughout our life experience when we have succeeded, even in small ways. By making a habit of recognizing our achievements, however big or small, we strengthen our self-confidence, and become better able to keep moving forward through both the highs and lows of life. Reshaping limiting beliefs into a more positive and empowering perspective can be exceptionally effective. Rather than entertaining thoughts of inadequacy, we have the ability to affirm to ourselves: "I am capable of learning and growing, and I am taking daily steps to improve my skills."

By nurturing a spirit of growth and development, we can gradually liberate ourselves from the constraints of these limiting beliefs and unleash our full potential.

Embracing a growth mindset is pivotal in surmounting limiting beliefs. It means eagerly embracing challenges, viewing failures as opportunities for growth, and nurturing the belief that we can continually enhance ourselves through effort and practice. Overcoming limiting beliefs is an ongoing process that requires dedication and persistence, but the rewards are immense both personally and in your business. Once you conquer your limiting beliefs, the next crucial step is to embrace change wholeheartedly.

Embracing Change

Change is not only inevitable; it is a constant force in entrepreneurship and in life. The ability to adapt and remain flexible in the face of change is essential for long-term success. Over the past few years, and especially in the aftermath of the pandemic, the value of adaptability in the face of change has not only become evident but has also emerged as a key factor distinguishing successful entrepreneurs from others. The first step in adapting to change is accepting its inevitability.

Many entrepreneurs fall into the trap of assuming that their current success, or failure, will persist indefinitely. However, markets are constantly evolving, customer preferences change, and unexpected events can disrupt even the most stable businesses. By acknowledging that change is an integral part of business, you can proactively prepare for it. A critical strategy for coping with change is staying proactive in identifying and responding to shifting market dynamics. This entails closely monitoring industry trends, listening to customer feedback, and seeking new growth opportunities. However, it's essential to differentiate between being reactive and being proactive.

.

Reactive entrepreneurs merely respond to situations as they arise, while proactive ones anticipate potential changes and take steps to prepare for them.

By staying ahead of the curve, you can seize emerging market opportunities and stay one step ahead of your competition. Maintaining flexibility and nimbleness is another essential strategy for effectively adapting to change. By cultivating both mental and physical adaptability, you can quickly adjust your business strategies in response to evolving market conditions. To evolve into a flexible and adaptable entrepreneur, it's essential to begin by gaining self-awareness and identifying your strengths and weaknesses. This can be done by cultivating a habit of continuous learning and proactively soliciting feedback from customers, employees, and mentors.

Once you embrace change as an inherent aspect of entrepreneurship, you become more receptive to the preliminary signs that change is about to occur, which diminishes the shock factor. You will also begin to welcome it because you realize that change inevitably paves the way for future growth and innovation. Remember, we aim to be proactive, rather than reactive, leaders. This means having a contingency plan for unexpected events, such as economic downturns, natural disasters, or industry disruptions which will effectively mitigate the impact of such events and ensure that your business can weather the storm.

If you consistently work on embracing the inevitability of change and mastering a proactive, creative, flexible and strategic mindset, you will position yourself for long-term success.

As the famous entrepreneur Mark Cuban said, "The only constant in business is change. Embrace it and grow, or resist it and die." I have always embraced change. This is in large part because my life experiences compelled me to nurture adaptability, openness, and nimbleness from a young age. As an entrepreneur, these learned traits are constantly put to the test. I remember a particular instance in 2017 after a devastating earthquake struck Mexico City and left many businesses in shambles. The damage was extensive, and we were forced to close our doors for several weeks. It was a period marked by darkness and uncertainty, but we knew that we had to stay nimble, open, and adaptable to change if we were going to make it through. One of the key strategies that helped us through this difficult time was to reframe our communication strategies both internally and externally. In the wake of the earthquake, it became apparent that our customers and employees were affected as well. Recognizing the importance of demonstrating empathy and support we shifted our marketing approach into a community-driven one. We focused on ways in which we could help our community and those impacted by the earthquake. We organized fundraisers and were able to create a sense of solidarity within our community and strengthen our connection with our customers.

Internally, our communication with our employees was also empathic. We understood that many of them were also struggling with the aftermath of the earthquake and needed support. We provided internal counseling services and made sure that they had access to resources to help them get back on their feet. This approach to communication created a sense of loyalty among our employees,who valued our efforts to stand by them during this challenging time. As we slowly began to rebuild our business, we remained committed to adaptability. We shifted our focus to offering more menu package options and expanded our menu to include more discount choices, knowing that our customers were looking for comforting foods and affordable options. In the end, our approach to communication and adaptability paid off. We were able to rebuild our business stronger than ever before, with a loyal customer base and dedicated employees. This experience taught me that sometimes the most challenging times can lead to the most significant growth, and it's important to stay open and adaptable to change to thrive in business.

As I look back I realize that the key to my success amidst change, was to fully embrace it.

This experience was a wake-up call, a reminder that even the most stable business can be upended by unexpected events. But instead of being paralyzed by fear, I chose to embrace the challenge and grow.

Turning Challenges into Opportunities

Creativity is a vital skill in today's ever-changing business landscape, it empowers you to generate innovative ideas and find ingenious solutions to obstacles. At its core, creativity entails thinking outside the box and exploring new possibilities. It requires an open and curious mindset, a willingness to take risks and experiment, and an ability to see things from different perspectives. Creativity is not just for artists or designers, it is an indispensable skill for all entrepreneurs, regardless of industry or background.

Think of it this way, a growth mindset will help you reframe your outlook on failure, change and adversity and creativity will allow you to transform those challenges into opportunities.

One of the most powerful ways that you can leverage creativity is by applying it to problem-solving. Creative problem-solving involves looking at challenges from different angles, exploring unconventional solutions, and breaking through mental barriers to find new and innovative approaches. Look at the success story of Zappos, where a creative idea transformed the online shoe retailer's fortunes. In the early days of the company, founder Tony Hsieh was struggling to differentiate his business from other online shoe retailers. One day, he had a creative idea: what if he offered free shipping both ways, and allowed customers to return shoes for any reason, no questions asked? This was a radical departure from traditional e-commerce practices, but it turned out to be a game-changer. Customers loved the convenience and flexibility of being able to try on shoes at home, and Zappos quickly became one of the most successful shoe retailers in the world. In your journey, remember to approach challenges with an open mind, curiosity, and a willingness to experiment.

How can you foster a creative mindset and harness its power for success? First and foremost, embracing failure as an opportunity to learn and grow is essential. Creativity inherently involves taking risks and venturing into uncharted territories. Entrepreneurs should reframe failure as an inevitable part of the creative process, recognizing that it provides valuable insights and propels them forward with a renewed determination. Cultivating curiosity is another pivotal aspect of nurturing creativity. Make a conscious effort to stay curious, open-minded, and embrace the pursuit of new experiences and perspectives. Engaging with diverse ideas and viewpoints can spark innovative thinking and lead to groundbreaking solutions.

Creativity thrives in collaboration; actively seek to build a network of collaborators, mentors, and advisors. These individuals can provide support, challenge your ideas, and infuse fresh perspectives that push the boundaries of your creativity. Fearlessness is also crucial in unleashing your creative potential. Do not shy away from experimentation, iteration, and refinement. Embrace the fact that creativity is a continuous process, not a one-time event. Be willing to test and adapt your ideas, continually refining them based on feedback and insights gained along the way.

Turning challenges into opportunities is an essential skill in the world of business. It is not uncommon for unexpected events to arise, potentially derailing progress and causing setbacks. One example I can give you is when my director of operations fell ill during our grand opening week. This presented a significant setback as this individual played a crucial role in overseeing our entire operations. It became evident that relying solely on one person for such a critical aspect of my business was considerably risky. However, rather than succumbing to panic, I viewed this situation as an opportunity to embrace the challenge and turn it into an opportunity. I rolled up my sleeves and took an active role. Although that week was somewhat hectic, during the course of the next few months I became an operations expert. I immersed myself in the operations, dedicating time to observe and learn every process. I closely studied the daily routines, developed comprehensive checklists and schedules, and introduced new processes to streamline our operations. I then documented everything and created an operations manual. By doing so, I ensured that the business would continue to run smoothly and efficiently despite the absence of any key team member. This experience taught me the importance of being prepared for unexpected events and viewing challenges as opportunities for growth and development.

The lesson I learned from this experience was invaluable: embracing challenges as opportunities can lead to both personal and professional growth. Rather than being daunted by unexpected setbacks, I now see them as opportunities to learn, adapt, and thrive. This mindset has not only strengthened our restaurant's operations but has also instilled in me a sense of confidence and resourcefulness as an entrepreneur. As I continued on my entrepreneurial journey, I felt armed with the knowledge that challenges can indeed be turned into stepping stones for success, no longer fearful of unforeseen events but rather viewing them as chances to innovate and evolve. This experience not only enhanced my leadership skills but also reinforced the belief in the power of a resilient mindset.

The Art of Resilience

Failure and change are constants in the business world and guess what, so is adversity. It's not a question of if you'll encounter adversity, but when. Whether it's a recession, a major setback, or a personal crisis, tough times are bound to occur. What distinguishes successful entrepreneurs from the rest is our ability to bounce back from adversity and keep moving forward despite the obstacles. This is where resilience comes in. Resilience is the ability to withstand and bounce back from adversity. It's not just about facing change and adversity; it's about being prepared for it. True resilience encompasses more than just inner strength; it also includes adaptability and a willingness to learn from tough experiences.

To be resilient, it is essential to cultivate a strong mindset, incorporate self-care practices, and develop specific strategies for staying motivated, and sustaining progress during challenging times.

Resilience is about building mental and emotional strength to persevere through the ups and downs of entrepreneurship and maintain a positive, solution-focused attitude.

Positive thinking and visualization are powerful tools to nurture resilience. Positive thinking involves training your mind to focus on the bright side of situations, and replacing any negative or pessimistic thoughts with more optimistic ones. By visualizing a positive outcome, you can change your mindset and your challenges with optimism and confidence. Creating a mental image of your desired outcome and choosing to continually focus on it can keep you motivated and determined, even in the face of setbacks and adversity.

Mindfulness and Self-Care

As an entrepreneur, it's easy to neglect our physical and emotional health, but despite the constant demands and pressures of the job, prioritizing one's health is crucial for maintaining a growth mindset and achieving long-term success.

When you are a business owner, you tend to put the interests of the business and your employees ahead of your own. In my case, I often neglected taking care of my emotional health. I was always too busy and too focused on prioritizing everything else above self care. Ironically, after I began devoting more time to mindfulness and self care, I noticed that everything within my business started to align and improve as well.

Embracing mindfulness can help you maintain focus on the present rather than becoming entangled in worries about the future or regrets about the past. This can lead to decreased stress levels and increased productivity and creativity. There are many different ways to practice mindfulness, including meditation, breathing exercises, and yoga.

Finding a mindfulness practice that works for you and incorporating it into your daily routine can help you maintain a resilient mindset and reduce stress.

One of the strategies that has proven highly effective for me is mindful breathing. I discovered that taking just a few minutes each day to sit quietly and focus on my breath can make a huge difference in reducing stress and improving focus. This is a simple practice that can be done anywhere, whether it's in my office before the start of a busy day, or in a quiet corner of the restaurant during a break.

Another strategy I use to stay grounded and focused is daily manifestations. This practice involves setting aside time each day to visualize my goals and intentions for the day ahead, helping me align my actions with my intentions. Whether it's achieving a business goal, focusing on finishing a task, or simply maintaining a positive attitude, this practice helps me to stay motivated and focused throughout the day.

Self-care which encompasses the nurturing of one's physical, mental, and emotional well-being, has proven indispensable for maintaining resilience and avoiding burnout. Self-care can include activities such as exercise, healthy eating, getting enough sleep, and taking breaks to recharge and engage in activities that you enjoy.

Entrepreneurs can easily overlook self-care in the pursuit of success, which can lead to burnout, reduced productivity, and even physical illness. Prioritizing self-care can help you maintain a resilient mindset and achieve long-term success.

Ever since I became aware of the significance and long-term impact of self care for both my business and personal well-being, I have made it a priority. This means making conscious choices about what I eat and drink, even when I'm busy and on-the-go. It means finding time to exercise regularly, whether it's hitting the gym before work or going for a run after a long day. It means making sure I get enough rest, even when there are a million things on my to do list.

Self care also means making time to recharge. I enjoy taking regular breaks throughout the day for activities like stretching, walking, or simply enjoying some music. To recharge my battery, I make it a priority to take longer breaks from my business every couple of months and take week-long trips. These breaks help me maintain my energy levels, so that I can continue to perform at my best.

Set Boundaries for a Balanced Life

Setting boundaries as a leader and entrepreneur means establishing clear limits and rules within your work and personal life. These boundaries help avoid burnout, maintain a balance between work and personal time, and make sure that you take care of yourself. By doing this, you empower yourself to confidently say no when necessary, channel your focus on important tasks, and communicate more effectively. It's a way to protect your overall well-being, stay focused on your goals, and bounce back from difficulties. As an entrepreneur I know this can be easier said than done but I can tell you from personal experience, if you choose to make it a priority you will see immediate and tangible results.

Prioritizing my well being has been paramount to helping me stay focused, productive, and fulfilled as an entrepreneur. While it's not always easy, making me a priority has allowed me to maintain balance in my life while running my business successfully.

Balancing work and personal life can be one of the most difficult challenges for business owners. It's easy to get caught up in the fast-paced, high-stress business environment of a restaurant and lose sight of what really matters. That's why I make a conscious effort to set boundaries between my work and personal life. For example, I always make sure to take at least one day off each week to spend quality time with my family and friends. I also make a conscious effort to leave work matters at work, resisting the urge to check emails or take work calls outside of business hours.

Celebrate the Small Victories

In addition to being mindful and practicing self-care, there are other strategies you can implement to stay motivated and maintain momentum in your business. A very effective strategy that I like to use is to break down big goals into smaller, more manageable tasks. By focusing on the quick wins, you can maintain a sense of progress and momentum, even when faced with major setbacks. As a seasoned entrepreneur, I've faced numerous significant challenges throughout my journey, but I've learned that breaking down complex objectives into actionable steps was key to achieving major milestones.

I vividly recall the seemingly overwhelming task of opening my flagship restaurant within just one month with only the assistance of my operations manager. The pressure was immense, and the clock was ticking relentlessly, so I chose a methodical approach. Instead of allowing ourselves to become overwhelmed, we chose to tackle the challenge one step at a time. We took the time to identify our key priorities, breaking them down into manageable tasks such as finding suppliers, assembling a team, and creating a marketing strategy. These were our main goals, and we meticulously laid them out into actionable steps. From researching potential vendors to designing a website and developing a content calendar, we focused on our daily progress through smaller, attainable achievements. By doing so, we maintained a sense of momentum and progress, even in the face of obstacles and setbacks.

Breaking down big goals not only kept us motivated but also allowed us to pivot efficiently when setbacks occurred. For example, when a key supplier fell through at the last minute, we were able to swiftly find a backup option due to the groundwork we had already laid out. The power of focusing on small wins cannot be underestimated, as it cultivated my growth mindset, ultimately leading to the successful inauguration of the flagship location.

Building a Support Network

Another strategy for nurturing your growth mindset is seeking support from others. As an entrepreneur, it's easy to fall into the trap of believing you must shoulder everything alone. However, no one can succeed entirely on their own. Building a strong support system is vital for weathering the ups and downs of business and cultivating a growth mindset. Networking is a foundational element of building a support system. Attending events and networking with fellow entrepreneurs and business leaders enables you to make valuable connections that can prove beneficial down the road. But networking isn't just about handing out business cards and making small talk; it's about building meaningful relationships with like-minded individuals who share your values and vision. Having mentors is another invaluable source of support. Experienced entrepreneurs can offer guidance, advice, and encouragement during challenging times. Seeking out mentors who have faced similar challenges in your industry can provide invaluable insights and help you navigate through obstacles. You can also build a robust inhouse support system by cultivating a positive and supportive team culture within your own business. As we discussed in chapter three, this starts with hiring the right people; individuals who share your values, work ethic, and vision for the company. But hiring individuals who share your values and work ethic is just the beginning; it's equally important to create an environment where people feel valued and supported. Open communication, growth opportunities, and recognition for hard work foster a cohesive and resilient team.

Remember that building a support system isn't just about what others can do for you; it's also about reciprocating and supporting others in their endeavors. By investing in others' success and building strong relationships, you create a network of mutual support and trust that will fortify your resilience and adaptability as an entrepreneur.

Believe in yourself and keep going. Even when you're making the right business decisions, your growth mindset will be tested. When I lost my restaurant brand after a four year legal battle I was devastated, but I refused to let it define me as a restaurateur. Instead, I garnered the support of my partner, the investors and my team and chose to take a risk and start again with a completely new brand. The challenges seemed insurmountable, from redesigning the concept and launching within a month, to positioning the new brand internally and externally. But by embracing the power of resilience and creativity, we successfully transformed those challenges into opportunities.

Looking back, I realize that having a resilient, adaptable, and growth mindset was the cornerstone to my success. It allowed me to take risks, pivot when necessary, and come out on top. I am now even more confident that no matter what challenges come my way, I will be able to overcome them and emerge even stronger.

Recipe for Success

As we reach the end of this book, have we truly addressed the question, What is the recipe for success? Is there a secret formula for running a profitable and sustainable business? Well, let me tell you, the ultimate key to your success lies within both you and your business. Success is the result of your everyday actions as you lead your team, it's linked to your data and how you leverage business intelligence to make business decisions. Success hinges on your ability to cultivate a resilient and adaptable growth mindset that embraces change and challenges with a positive outlook. The recipe for success has always been an intrinsic part of you. While I have shared the technical aspects of managing a profitable restaurant, it is important to understand that mere business knowledge and the implementation of the strategies in this book alone can not guarantee complete success. Because success involves more, it involves peace and freedom in your personal life as well. Success is not just about having a profitable business but leading a balanced life that you get to live on your own terms. At the end of the day, what's the point of running a profitable restaurant if you are sacrificing your personal life and enduring constant stress?

Success is a life-long journey, not a final destination.

As you embark on your own success journey, cultivate your growth mindset by fearlessly embracing failure as an opportunity to learn and grow, nurture your curiosity to explore uncharted territories, build a supportive network that uplifts and challenges you, and continually challenge your ideas. Let your passion and determination be the driving forces that push you forward, even in the face of uncertainty. Your journey as an entrepreneur will be filled with both successes and setbacks, but remember that success is not a final destination but rather a continuous journey of growth and learning. As you face each challenge with resilience and creativity, you will realize that every setback is, in fact, an opportunity for growth and more success. Embrace this journey wholeheartedly, and you will find that the fulfillment of your dreams lies not only in reaching your goals but also in the progress you make and the person you become along the way. So, here's to your remarkable success journey as an entrepreneur!

Next Steps

Feeling empowered and inspired?
If so, join Restaurant Killers.

Restaurant Killers was born out of a deep understanding of the challenges restaurateurs face in an industry that often feels like a relentless adversary. Our mission is to empower restaurateurs like you, to break free from the industry's grip, regain control of your businesses, and finally live life on your own terms. The industry's high failure rate and competitive culture has cast a shadow over the dreams of countless restaurateurs. We see the burnout, the sacrifice, and the unfulfilled aspirations. It is time for change. Restaurant Killers emerges as a powerful force for transformation.

Our brand stands for unity against the industry's shortcomings. We're rewriting the narrative of what it means to run a restaurant. Success should no longer be reserved for the privileged few with connections, degrees and guarded industry insights. We strongly believe that passion, education, and a data-driven approach to business should be the cornerstones of success. We are fostering a community of collaboration and knowledge exchange. We're breaking down the walls of isolation that many restaurateurs face, providing a platform for real solutions and actionable strategies. We aren't just a name, we are a movement.

We're here to guide you on the path to successful business ownership that doesn't demand the sacrifice of your personal life.

Your story is important to us. Write a blog on our website, share your story, write a review of the book and follow us on social media. Join us in rewriting your story. Say goodbye to burnout, uncertainty, and imbalance. Embrace a network that empowers you and a future that's defined by your success as both a restaurateur and a fulfilled individual. Your transformation begins today.

www.ingramcontent.com/pod-product-compliance
Lightning Source LLC
Chambersburg PA
CBHW071650200326
41519CB00012BA/2466